A Practical Guide for Translators

TOPICS IN TRANSLATION
Series Editors: Susan Bassnett, *University of Warwick, UK*
Edwin Gentzler, *University of Massachusetts, Amherst, USA*
Editor for Translation in the Commercial Environment:
Geoffrey Samuelsson-Brown, *University of Surrey, UK*

Other Books in the Series
Annotated Texts for Translation: English – French
  Beverly Adab
Annotated Texts for Translation: English – German
  Christina Schäffner with Uwe Wiesemann
Constructing Cultures: Essays on Literary Translation
  Susan Bassnett and André Lefevere
Contemporary Translation Theories (2nd Edition)
  Edwin Gentzler
Culture Bumps: An Empirical Approach to the Translation of Allusions
  Ritva Leppihalme
Frae Ither Tongues: Essays on Modern Translations into Scotts
  Bill Findlay (ed.)
Linguistic Auditing
  Nigel Reeves and Colin Wright
Literary Translation: A Practical Guide
  Clifford E. Landers
Paragraphs on Translation
  Peter Newmark
The Coming Industry of Teletranslation
  Minako O'Hagan
The Interpreter's Resource
  Mary Phelan
The Pragmatics of Translation
  Leo Hickey (ed.)
Translation and Nation: A Cultural Politics of Englishness
  Roger Ellis and Liz Oakley-Brown (eds)
Translation-mediated Communication in a Digital World
  Minako O'Hagan and David Ashworth
Time Sharing on Stage: Drama Translation in Theatre and Society
  Sirkku Aaltonen
Words, Words, Words. The Translator and the Language Learner
  Gunilla Anderman and Margaret Rogers

Other Books of Interest
More Paragraphs on Translation
  Peter Newmark
Translation in a Global Village
  Christina Schäffner (ed.)
Translation Research and Interpreting Research
  Christina Schäffner (ed.)
Translation Today: Trends and Perspectives
  Gunilla Anderman and Margaret Rogers (eds)

Please contact us for the latest book information:
Multilingual Matters, Frankfurt Lodge, Clevedon Hall,
Victoria Road, Clevedon, BS21 7HH, England
http://www.multilingual-matters.com

TOPICS IN TRANSLATION 25
Editor for Translation in the Commercial Environment:
Geoffrey Samuelsson-Brown

A Practical Guide for Translators

(Fourth Edition)

Geoffrey Samuelsson-Brown

MULTILINGUAL MATTERS LTD
Clevedon • Buffalo • Toronto

Library of Congress Cataloging in Publication Data
Samuelsson-Brown, Geoffrey
A Practical Guide for Translators/Geoffrey Samuelsson-Brown, 4th ed.
Topics in Translation: 25
Includes bibliographical references and index.
1. Translating and interpreting. I. Title. II. Series.
P306.S25 2004
418'.02--dc22   2003024118

British Library Cataloguing in Publication Data
A catalogue entry for this book is available from the British Library.

ISBN 1-85359-730-9 (hbk)
ISBN 1-85359-729-5 (pbk)

Multilingual Matters Ltd
UK: Frankfurt Lodge, Clevedon Hall, Victoria Road, Clevedon BS21 7HH.
USA: UTP, 2250 Military Road, Tonawanda, NY 14150, USA.
Canada: UTP, 5201 Dufferin Street, North York, Ontario M3H 5T8, Canada.

Typeset by Archetype-IT Ltd (http://www.archetype-it.com).
Printed and bound in Great Britain by the Cromwell Press Ltd.

Contents

'Oh, so you're a translator – that's interesting!'   A day in the life of a
translator   Finding a 'guardian angel'   Literary or non-literary
translator?   Translation and interpreting   Starting life as a translator   Work
experience placements as a student   Becoming a translator by
circumstance   Working as a staff translator   Considering a job
application   Working as a freelance   What's the difference between a translation
company and a translation agency?   Working directly with clients   Test
translations   Recruitment competitions

Target language and source language   Target language deprivation   Retaining a
sharp tongue   Localisation   Culture shocks   Stereotypes

Who should you get to translate?   The service provider and the uninformed
buyer   How to find a translation services provider   Is price any guide to
quality?   Communication with the translation services provider

Starting a business   Is translation a financially-rewarding career?   Support
offered to new businesses   Counting words   Quotations   Working from
home   Private or business telephone line?   Holidays   Safety nets   Dealing with
salesmen   Advertising   Financial considerations   Marketing and developing
your services   OK, where do you go from here?

Foreword to the Fourth Edition

The fourth edition of *A Practical Guide for Translators*, which is now available, sees the training and work situation of translators much changed from when the book first appeared on the market.

In 1993, when the first edition was published, educational institutions in the UK had only started to acknowledge that in order for linguists to turn into translators training was needed at the academic level. Courses were gradually becoming available in order to prepare the student translator for the professional demands to be met by the functioning practitioner. Although the Institute of Linguists and its Postgraduate Diploma in Translation had already pointed to the requirements inherent in the profession, with the setting up of the Institute of Translation and Interpreting in 1986, the need for the special linguistic skills of the translator was further highlighted.

This new edition of the book finds practising translators as a firmly established group of professionals, much helped by the advice and guidance over the years of previous editions of the book advising on how to bridge the gap between academic training and real-life experience; it is a task for which Geoff Samuelsson-Brown is uniquely equipped, being himself a practising translator and the former manager of a translation company.

At the present moment, the dawn of the twenty-first century places new demands on the translator, the result of conflicting economic and linguistic developments. The need for in-house translators is giving way to a rapidly increasing use of freelance translators for whom awareness of the demands of setting up in business becomes imperative.

In a wider European context, as membership of new nations with speakers of languages less commonly known beyond their national borders will result in further growth of the EU, so will the need for translators. Also growing in strength is the might of English as the *lingua franca* of Europe and the means of global communication. In the near future, translators are likely to face new challenges; as technical writers and editors they will soon be asked to augment their roles as translators and to further widen the scope of their present work as language mediators.

A PRACTICAL GUIDE FOR TRANSLATORS

For many years a contributor to the undergraduate and postgraduate programmes in Translation Studies as well as to professional development courses offered to practising translators by the Centre for Translation Studies at the University of Surrey, Geoff Samuelsson-Brown's cutting edge experience in forming the fourth edition of *A Practical Guide for Translators*, will be of benefit to anyone with an interest in translation, on course to become an even more highly skilled profession in the years to come.

Gunilla Anderman

Professor of Translation Studies
Centre for Translation Studies
University of Surrey

Preface to the Fourth Edition

'The wisest of the wise may err.'
Aeschylus, 525–456 BC

In the early 1990s, after teaching Translation Studies at the University of Surrey for seven years at undergraduate and postgraduate level, I felt there was a need for practical advice to complement linguistics and academic theory. 'A Practical Guide for Translators' grew from this idea. The first edition was published in April 1993 and I have been heartened by the response it has received from its readers and those who have reviewed it. I am most grateful for the comments received and have been mindful of these when preparing this and previous revisions.

I started translation as a full-time occupation in 1982 even though I had worked as a technical writer, editor and translator since 1974. In the time since I have worked as a staff translator and freelance as well as starting and building up a translation company that I sold in 1999. This has given me exposure to different aspects of translation both as a practitioner, project manager and head of a translation company. It is on this basis that I would like to share my experience. You could say that I have gone full circle because I now accept assignments as a freelance since I enjoy the creativity that working as a translator gives. I also have an appreciation of what goes on after the freelance has delivered his translation to an agency or client.

Trying to keep pace of technology is a daunting prospect. In the first edition of the book I recommended a minimum hard disk size of 40 MB. My present computer (three years old yet still providing sterling service) has a hard disk of 20 GB, Pentium III processor, CD rewriter, DVD, ISDN communication and fairly sophisticated audio system. My laptop has a similar specification that would have been difficult to imagine only a few years ago and is virtually a mobile office! When looking through past articles that I have written, I came across a comparison that I made between contemporary word processors and the predecessors of today's personal computers. The following table is reproduced from that article. DFE is the name of a word processor whereas the others are, what I called at the time, micro processors. This was written in 1979.

The DFE I purchased in 1979 cost around £5,400 then but was a major advance

System	RAM (kB)	Disk capacity		Software included		
		standard (kB)	optional (kB)	Text processing	Data retrieval	Maths
Commodore (Wordcraft 80)	32	950	22	Yes	No	No
Eagle (Spellbinder)	64	769	–	Yes	Limited	No
Olympia (BOSS)	64	2 × 140	1 × 600 + 1 × 5 MB	Yes	No	No
DFE	64	2 × 121	up to 192 MB	Yes	Yes	Yes

compared with correctable golfball typewriters. Just imagine what £5,400 would be at net present value and the computing power you could buy for the money.

New to this edition is looking in more detail at the business aspects of translation. Legislation on terms payment for work has been introduced in the United Kingdom which I welcome. So many freelance translators have terms imposed on them by clients (these include translation agencies and companies!). More of this in in Chapter 4 – Running a translation business. I have also endeavoured to identify changes in information technology that benefit the translator – I find being able to use the internet for research an excellent tool. The fundamental concept of the book remains unchanged however in that it is intended for those who have little or no practical experience of translation in a commercial environment. Some of the contents may be considered elementary and obvious. I have assumed that the reader has a basic knowledge of personal computers.

I was tempted to list useful websites in the Appendix but every translator has his own favourites. Mine have a Scandinavian bias since I translate from Danish, Norwegian and Swedish into English so I have resisted the temptation. I have given the websites of general interest in the appropriate sections of the book.

The status of the translator has grown but the profession is still undervalued despite a growing awareness of the need for translation services. The concept of 'knowledge workers' has appeared in management speak. The mere fact that you may be able to speak a foreign language does not necessarily mean that you are able to translate. (This does not mean, however, that oral skills are not necessary. Being able to communicate verbally is a distinct advantage.) Quite often you will be faced with the layman's question, 'How many languages do you speak?'. It is quite possible to translate a language without being able to speak it – a fact that may surprise some people. Translation is also creative and not just an automatic process. By this I mean that you will need to exercise your interpreting and editing skills since, in many cases, the person who has written the source text may not have been entirely clear in what he has written. It is then your job as a translator to endeavour to understand what the writer wishes to say and then express that clearly in the target language.

An issue that has become more noticeable in the last few years is the deterioration in the quality of the source text provided for translation. There may be many reasons for this but all present difficulties to the translator trying to fully understand the text provided for translation. The lack of comprehension is not because of the translator's level of competence and skills but lack of quality control by the author of the original text. The difficulty is often compounded by the translator not being able communicate directly with the author to resolve queries.

Documentation on any product or service is often the first and perhaps only opportunity for presenting what a company, organisation or enterprise is trying to sell. Ideally, documentation should be planned at the beginning of a product's or service's development – not as a necessary attachment once the product or service is ready to be marketed. Likewise, translation should not be something that is thought of at the very last minute.

Documentation and translation are an integral part of a product or service and, as a consequence, must be given due care, time and attention. As an example, Machinery Directive 98/37/EC/EEC specifies that documentation concerned with health and safety etc. needs to be in an officially recognised language of the country where the product will be used. In fact, payment terms for some products or services often include a statement that payment is subject to delivery of proper documentation.

In addition to the language and subject skills possessed by a translator, he needs skills in the preparation of documentation in order to produce work that is both linguistically correct and aesthetically pleasing.

The two most important qualifications you need as a translator are being able to express yourself fluently in the target language (your language of habitual use) and having an understanding of the text you are translating. To these you could usefully add qualifications in specialist subjects. The skills you need as a translator are considered in Figure 1 on Page 2.

There are two principal categories of translators – literary and non-literary. These categorisations are not entirely accurate but are generally accepted. The practical side of translation is applicable to both categories although the ways of approaching subjects are different. Since the majority of translators are non-literary, and I am primarily a non-literary translator, I feel confident that the contents of this book can provide useful advice. Most of the book is however relevant to both categories.

Those who are interested specifically in literary translation will find Clifford E.

Landers' book '*Literary Translation – A Practical Guide*' extremely useful and readworthy.

Many books have been written on the theory of translation and are, by their very nature, theoretical rather than practical. Others have been written as compilations of conference papers. These are of interest mainly to established translators and contain both theory and practical guidance.

The use of he/him/his in this book is purely a practical consideration and does not imply any gender discrimination on my part.

It is very easy for information to become outdated. It is therefore inevitable that some of the details and prices will have been superseded by the time you read this book. Comparison is however useful.

This book endeavours to give the student or fledgling translator an insight into the 'real' world of translation. I have worked as a staff translator, a freelance and as head of a translation company. I also spent around ten years in total as an associate lecturer at the University of Surrey. I hope the contents of this book will save the reader making some of the mistakes that I've made.

When burning the midnight oil to meet the publisher's deadline for submission of this book, I am painfully aware of all its limitations. Every day I read or hear about items I would like to have included. It would have been tempting to write about the structure and formatting of a website, running a translation company, the management of large translation projects in several languages, management strategy, international business culture and a host of other related issues.

By not doing so I could take the cynical attitude that this will give the critics something to hack away at but that would be unkind. I will have to console myself that now is the time to start work on the next edition. I am reminded of John Steinbeck's words with which, I am sure, every translator will sympathise.

'*To finish is sadness to a writer – a little death. He puts the last words down and it is done. But it isn't really done. The story goes on and leaves the writer behind, for no story is ever done.*'

Geoffrey Samuelsson-Brown
Bracknell, July 2003

Acknowledgements

This book has been compiled with the help of colleagues and friends who have given freely of their time and have provided information as well as valuable assistance.

I am grateful to the following for permission to reproduce extracts from various publications:

British Standards Institute, The Building Services Research and Information Association, and the Volvo Car Corporation.

Extract from 'The Guinness Book of Records 1993', Copyright © Guinness Publishing Limited.

The Institute of Translation and Interpreting; The Institute of Linguists; and the Fédération Internationale de Traducteurs for permission to quote freely from the range of publications issued by these professional associations for translators.

ASLIB, for permission to use extracts from chapters that originally appeared in 'The Translator's Handbook', 1996, Copyright © Aslib and contributors, edited by Rachel Owens.

Special thanks go to Gordon Fielden, past Secretary of the Translators' Association of the Society of Authors, for allowing me to reproduce extracts from his informative papers on copyright in translation.

Last, but not least, thanks as always to my wife and best mate Geraldine (who is not a translator – two in the family would probably be intolerable!) for acting as a guinea pig, asking questions about the profession that I had not even considered. Thanks also for lending a sympathetic ear and a psychologist's analytical viewpoint when I've gone off at a tangent.

1 How to become a translator

'They know enough who know how to learn.'
Henry Adams, 1836–1918

People usually become translators in one of two ways. Either by design or by circumstance. There are no formal academic qualifications required to work as a translator but advertisements for translators in the press and professional journals tend to ask for graduates with professional qualifications and three years' experience.

Many countries have professional organisations for translators and if the organisation is a member of the Fédération Internationale des Traducteurs (FIT) it will have demonstrated that it sets specific standards and levels of academic achievement for membership. The translation associations affiliated to FIT can be found on FIT's website – www.fit-ift.org. Two organisations in the United Kingdom set examinations for professional membership. These are the Institute of Linguists and the Institute of Translation and Interpreting. To gain a recognised professional qualification through membership of these associations you must meet certain criteria. Comprehensive details of professional associations for translators in the United Kingdom are given in Chapter 10.

If you have completed your basic education and have followed a course of study to become a translator, you will then need to gain experience. As a translator, you will invariably be asked to translate every imaginable subject. The difficulty is accepting the fact that you have limitations since you are faced with the dilemma of *'How do I gain experience if I don't accept translations or do I accept translations to get the experience?'*. Ideally as a fledgling translator you should work under the guidance of a more experienced colleague.

1.1 'Oh, so you're a translator – that's interesting!'

An opening gambit at a social or business gathering is for the person next to you to ask what you do. When the person finds out your profession the inevitable response is, 'Oh so you're a translator – that's interesting' and, before you have chance to say anything, the next rejoinder is, 'I suppose you translate things like books and letters into foreign

1

languages, do you?'. Without giving you a chance to utter a further word you are hit by the fatal catch-all, 'Still, computers will be taking over soon, won't they?'. When faced with such a verbal attack you hardly have the inclination to respond.

The skills clusters that the translator needs at his fingertips are shown below.

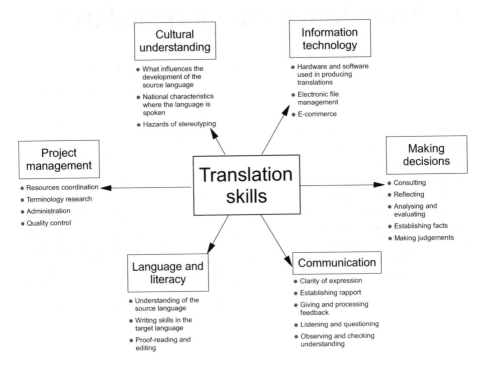

Figure 1. Translation skills clusters

Regrettably, an overwhelming number of people – and these include clients – harbour many misconceptions of what is required to be a skilled translator. Such misconceptions include:

- As a translator you can translate all subjects
- If you speak a foreign language *ipso facto* you can automatically translate into it
- If you can hold a conversation in a foreign language then you are bilingual
- Translators are mind-readers and can produce a perfect translation without having to consult the author of the original text, irrespective of whether it is ambiguous, vague or badly written

- No matter how many versions of the original were made before final copy was approved or how long the process took, the translator needs only one stab at the task, and very little time, since he gets it right first time without the need for checking or proof-reading. After all, the computer does all that for you.

1.2   A day in the life of a translator

Each day is different since a translator, particularly a freelance, needs to deal with a number of tasks and there is no typical day. I usually get up at around 7 in the morning, shower, have breakfast and get to my desk at around 8 just as my wife is leaving to drive to her office. Like most freelances I have my office at home.

I work in spells of 50 minutes and take a break even if it's just to walk around the house. I try and take at least half an hour for lunch and try to finish at around 5 unless there is urgent work and then I will perhaps work in the evening for an hour or so. But I do the latter only if a premium payment is offered and I wish to accept the work. I spend one day a week during term time as an associate university lecturer.

If I were to analyse an average working month of 22 possible working days I would get the following:

Task or item to which time is accounted	Time spent on the task
Translation including project management, research, draft translation, proof reading and editing, resolving queries and administration	Thirteen and a half days
Researching and preparing lectures, setting and marking assignments, travelling to university, administration and lecturing. (This is based on teaching around 28 weeks in the academic year)	Two days
Office administration including invoicing, purchasing and correspondence (tax issues and book-keeping are dealt with by my accountant)	Two days
External activities such as networking and marketing	One day
Continuous personal development including – and this is not a joke – watching relevant TV programmes or reading articles on subjects in which you have or wish to improve your expertise.	One day
Public or other holidays (say 21 days leave and 7 days public holidays)	Two and a half

My average monthly output for these thirteen and a half effective days is around 34,000 words. If this is spread out over effective working days of 8 working hours (8   50

3

minutes in reality), my effective hourly production rate is 315 words an hour. This may not seem a lot but it may be worth considering that to expect to work undisturbed on translation eight hours a day, five days a week, is unrealistic. There may also be times when you are physically or mentally unable to work – how do you take account of such eventualities as a freelance?

1.3   Finding a 'guardian angel'

Under the Institute of Translation and Interpreting's mentoring or 'guardian angel' scheme, you as a fledgling translator will have the opportunity to measure yourself against realistic standards through contact with established translators at the ITI's workshops, seminars and at continuing education courses covering practical as well as linguistic matters. Under the ITI Mentoring Scheme you can ask for advice from an established translator working into the same language as yourself and who will take a personal interest in you at the beginning of your career.

The kind of points on which he can advise will be:

- The presentation of your work, reasonable deadlines, whether to insert translator's notes, how literal or how free your translations should be; what rates you can expect or demand; word, line or page counts.
- What is the minimum equipment you need to start up in the profession? Which dictionaries and reference books are really useful and worth buying (and which are not)? Is it worth advertising your services and, if so, how?
- Producing a good job application; job interview techniques; telephone manner; invoicing your work.
- Helpful, kind and honest feedback on the quality of a piece of work you have done, recognising your strengths and advising what you can do about any limitations you may have.

A guardian angel cannot employ you or find you work directly, but he should be able to help to acquire a more realistic idea of what the work entails. He can also be supportive and positive in appraising your good and not-quite-so-good points and suggesting ways of overcoming your initial difficulties.

1.4   Literary or non-literary translator?

Though used quite generally, these terms are not really satisfactory. They do however indicate a differentiation between translators who translate books for publication (including non-fiction works) and those who translate texts for day-to-day commercial, technical or legal purposes.

1.4.1　What is literary translation?

Literary translation is one of the four principal categories of translator. The others are interpreting, scientific and technical, and commercial/business translation. There are also specialist fields within these categories. Literary translation is not confined to the translation of great works of literature. When the Copyright Act refers to 'literary works' it places no limitations on their style or quality. All kinds of books, plays, poems, short stories and writings are covered, including such items as a collection of jokes, the script of a documentary, a travel guide, a science textbook and an opera libretto.

Becoming a successful literary translator is not easy. It is far more difficult to get established, and financial rewards, at the bottom of the scale, are not excessive by any measure. Just reward is seldom given to the translator – for example, the translator of Thomas Mann's 'Death in Venice' doesn't even get a mention. Your rewards in terms of royalties depend on the quality and success of your translation. You would be well-advised to contact the Translators Association of the Society of Authors on matters such as royalties, copyright and translation rights.

1.4.2　Qualities rather than qualifications

When experienced members of the Translators Association were asked to produce a profile of a literary translator, they listed the following points:

- the translator needs to have a feeling for language and a fascination with it,
- the translator must have an intimate knowledge of the source language and of the regional culture and literature, as well as a reasonable knowledge of any special subject that is dealt with in the work that is being published,
- the translator should be familiar with the original author's other work,
- the translator must be a skilled and creative writer in the target language and nearly always will be a native speaker of it,
- the translator should always be capable of moving from one style to another in the language when translating different works,
- the aim of the translator should be to convey the meaning of the original work as opposed to producing a mere accurate rendering of the words,
- the translator should be able to produce a text that reads well, while echoing the tone and style of the original – as if the original author were writing in the target language.

As is evident from this description, the flair, skill and experience that are required by a good literary translator resembles the qualities that are needed by an 'original' writer. It is not surprising that writing and translating often go hand in hand.

1.4.3   Literary translation as a career

Almost without exception, translators of books, plays, etc. work on a freelance basis. In most cases they do not translate the whole of a foreign language work 'on spec': they go ahead with the translation only after the publisher or production company has undertaken to issue/perform the translation, and has signed an agreement commissioning the work and specifying payment.

As in all freelance occupations, it is not easy for the beginner to ensure a constant flow of commissions. Only a few people can earn the equivalent of a full salary from literary translation alone. Literary translators may have another source of income, for example from language teaching or an academic post. They may combine translation with running a home. They may write books themselves as well as translating other authors' work. They may be registered with a translation agency and possibly accept shorter (and possibly more lucrative) commercial assignments between longer stretches of literary translation.

If you are considering a career in literary translation, it is worth reading a companion to this book. It is entitled *Literary Translation – A Practical Guide* (Ref. 1) and is written by Clifford E. Landers.

Clifford E. Landers writes with the clean, refreshing style that puts him on a par with Bill Bryson. His book should be read by all translators – not only because it is full of practical advice to would-be and practicing literary translators but also because it has a fair number of parallels with non-literary translation.

The title embodies Practical and this is precisely what the book is about. Practical aspects include The translator's tools, Workspace and work time, Financial matters, Contracts. These words of wisdom should be read and inwardly digested by all translators – Yes, even we non-literary translators who seldom come in serious contact with the more creative members of our genre. Literary translators have a much harder job, at least in the early stages of their careers, in getting established. You probably won't find commissioners of literary translations in the Yellow Pages. In this context Clifford Landers provides useful information on getting published and related issues such as copyright.

Selectively listing the contents is an easy but useful way of giving a five-second overview and, in addition to what it mentioned above, the book also considers Why Literary Translation? (*answered in a concise and encouraging manner*), Getting started, Preparing to translate, Staying on track, What literary translators really translate, The care and feeding of authors, Some notes on translating poetry, Puns and word play, Pitfalls and how to avoid them, Where to publish and so much more.

1.5   Translation and interpreting

The professions of translation and interpreting are significantly different but there are areas where the two overlap. As a translator I interpret the written word and the result of my interpretation is usually in written form. I have time to deliberate, conduct research, proof-read, revise, consult colleagues and submit my written translation to my client. An interpreter interprets the spoken word and does not have the luxury of time nor a second chance to revise the result of the interpretation. Many translators will have done some interpreting but this will probably have been incidental to written translation.

To find out more about the profession of translation I would recommend you read *The Interpreter's Resource* (Ref. 2) written by Mary Phelan. This book provides an overview of language interpreting at the turn of the twenty-first century and is an invaluable tool for aspiring and practicing interpreters. This guide (with the accent on practical) begins with a brief history of interpreting and then goes on to explain key terms and the contexts in which they are used. The chapter on community interpreting details the situation regarding community, court and medical interpreting around the world. As with any other profession, ethics are important and this book includes five original Codes of Ethics from different professional interpreter organisations.

While this discussion could migrate to other areas where language skills are used, another form of translation is that of forensic linguistics. My experience of this, and that of colleagues, is listening to recordings of telephone calls to provide evidence that can be used during criminal or disciplinary proceedings. This can present an interesting challenge when various means such as slang or dialect are used in an attempt to conceal incriminating evidence.

But let's get back to translation.

1.6   Starting life as a translator

A non-literary translator needs to offer a technical, commercial or legal skill in addition to being able to translate. Fees for freelance work are usually received fairly promptly and are charged at a fixed rate – usually per thousand words of source text.

If you are just starting out in life as a translator, and have not yet gained recognised professional qualifications (through the Institute of Linguists, the Institute of Translation and Interpreting, or some other recognised national body) or experience, you may be fortunate in getting a job as a junior or trainee staff translator under the guidance and watchful eye of a senior experienced colleague. This will probably be with a translation company or other organisation that needs the specific skills of a translator.

Having a guide and mentor at an early stage is invaluable. There's a lot more to translation than just transferring a text from one language to another, as you will soon discover.

You will possibly have spent an extended period in the country where the language of your choice is spoken. Gaining an understanding of the people, their culture and national characteristics at first hand is a vital factor. There is the argument of course that you can translate a language you may not be able to speak. This applies to languages that are closely related. For example, if you have gained fluency in French you may find that you are able to translate Spanish. This is perhaps stretching the point though.

What do you do when faced with slang words, dialect words, trade or proprietary names? This is when an understanding of the people as well as the language is useful. If you have worked or lived in the country where the source language is spoken, it is very useful to be able to contact people if you have difficulties with obscure words that are not in standard dictionaries. If the word or words can be explained in the source language, you have a better chance of being able to provide a correct translation.

You will inevitably be doing your work on a computer. Have the patience to learn proper keyboarding skills by mastering the ability to touch type. Your earning capacity will be in direct proportion to your typing speed and, once you have taken the trouble to learn this skill properly, your capacity will far outstrip the 'two-finger merchants'. Of all the practical skills you need to learn as a translator, I would consider this one of the most essential and directly rewarding.

Let's summarise the desirable requirements for becoming a translator by design:

- education to university level by attaining your basic degree in modern languages or linguistics
- spending a period in the country where the language of your choice is spoken
- completing a postgraduate course in translation studies
- gaining some knowledge or experience of the subjects you intend translating
- getting a job as a trainee or junior translator with a company
- learning to touch type
- the willingness to commit to lifelong learning.

This gets you onto the first rung of the ladder.

1.7 Work experience placements as a student

The opportunities for work experience placements as a student are difficult to find but extremely valuable if you are fortunate enough to get one. The company that I managed considered applications to determine if there was a suitable candidate and appropriate work that could be offered. On the following pages is an example of a memo issued with an eight-week programme designed to offer a French university student broad exposure to what goes on in a translation company.

There are, of course, routine tasks that everybody has to do – these include photo-copying and word counting. Make sure that a structured programme is offered, that you are not being used as a dogsbody, and that you derive benefit from the experience.

Since the company offering the placement will incur costs as a result, not least by providing a member of staff as a supervisor and facilities for you to use, you as a student on placement should not expect to receive a salary even though some discretionary

1996 Summer placement programme – Cécile X

Distribution: *All staff*

Introduction

The purpose of this Summer placement with ATS Limited is to provide Cécile with a broad exposure to the different operations that are performed at a translation company, and an appreciation that being a translator is a very demanding and exacting profession.

Where applicable, the relevant procedures in ATS's Quality Manual shall be studied in parallel with the different operations, e.g. ATS/OPS 02 Translator Selection. Comments should be invited on the comprehensibility of the procedures by an uninitiated reader.

Cécile will be here from 1 July – 31 August and her supervisor will be FS. This responsibility will be shared with those looking after Cécile in the various sections:

- *Production coordination – KN*
- *Proof-reading and quality control – AL and SM*
- *Administration – JA*
- *Freelance translator assessment – MS*

I'm sure that all members of staff will do their best to make Cécile's stay with us both enjoyable and rewarding.

Information to be provided

Information pack about the company to include:

- *ATS's leaflet in English*
- *Organisation chart*
- *Copy of 'A Practical Guide for Translators'*

Other information will be provided by the various section supervisors.

Translation, proof-reading and editing

- *Familiarisation with the C-C project.*
- *Reviewing ATS's presentation slides in French*
- *checking overheads produced by SH. Emphasis on the importance of accuracy.*

(continued)

9

Read through SRDE manual in French and English to provide a concept of what is involved.

- *One-to-One session with SM on the different types of proof reading:*
  - *proof-reading marks as per BS 5261*
  - *scan-check for information purposes only*
  - *full checking*
  - *checking for publication*
  - *checking documents for legal certification*

Database management

MS will provide an introduction to database management and the way freelance translators are selected. The emphasis shall be on stringent criteria for selection and the way in which the information is managed.

KN will supervise an introduction to the way database management is used as a tool in production coordination.

Project management

JA and KN will provide an introduction to project management and its significance as a key factor for success in a translation company. This will include:

- *Familiarisation with the quality control and project management aspects of Client XXXX*
- *Project management of Client YYYY assignments*
- *Administration associated with an assignment from initial inquiry to when the work is sent to the client*
- *Use of different communication media such as fax and electronic mail.*

Library and information retrieval

A familiarisation with ATS's library and its collection of dictionaries, glossaries, text books, reference books, company literature and past translations will be provided by HJ.

(continued)

General administration

Cécile will be delegated routine administration tasks such as photocopying and word counting.

Client visits

If the opportunity arises, and if deemed relevant, Cécile will be invited to accompany members of staff on client visits as an observer. Clients will be contacted in advance to seek their approval.

Weekly reviews

FS will hold weekly reviews with Cécile to assess progress and seek solutions to any problems.

Bracknell, 28 June, 1996

payment may be made. You can gain considerable benefit through meeting experienced practitioners and seeing what goes on in a translation company. You may decide after the placement that translation is not for you. You then have a chance of redirecting your studies.

1.8 Becoming a translator by circumstance

Becoming a translator in this way is a different kettle of fish. The advantage in this case is that the person concerned will usually have gained several years' experience in a chosen profession before translation appears as an option. Many people become translators when working abroad, either with their company as a result of being posted to a foreign country or after having married a foreign national and moving to an adopted country. Probably the best way to learn a language is to live in the country where the language is spoken. The disadvantage is perhaps the lack of linguistic theory that will have been gained by a person with a formal education in this discipline.

Are you suitable as a translator? I suppose the only answer is to actually try a translation and see how you feel about it. In my own case, I was working in Sweden as a technical editor in a company's technological development centre using English as a working language. I did some translation as part of my work and it is from this beginning that my interest in the profession grew.

Working as a freelance translator is a fairly lonely occupation. The work is intense at times, particularly when you are up against very tight deadlines. Translators tend not to be gregarious.

Initially it is tempting to tackle all subjects. Ignorance can be bliss, but risky. After all, how do you gain experience if you don't do the work? I suppose it is rather like being an actor – if you're not a member of Equity you can't get a job and, if you don't have a job, you can't apply to join Equity. (An interesting but not quite parallel situation is that of the non-Japanese sumo wrestler Konishiki. Despite having won the requisite number of tournaments to become a *yokozuna* or Grand Champion, Konishiki lacks the vital element essential to become a Grand Champion sumo wrestler – a quality called *hinkaku*. Loosely translated, it means 'dignity-class' and it is sumo's Catch 22. To become successful in sumo, you need to have *hinkaku*. But since only Japanese are supposed to understand the true meaning of *hinkaku*, only Japanese can become Grand Champions.)

You will have enough problems to wrestle with but the opportunity to work as a staff translator will smooth your path.

1.9   Working as a staff translator

Before you consider working as a freelance, you would be well advised to gain at least a couple of years' experience as a staff translator – if you are fortunate in being offered a position. This offers a number of advantages:

- An income from day 1 and a structured career path.
- On-the-job skills development under the watchful eye of an experienced translator or editor. This will save you many attempts at re-inventing the wheel.
- Access to the reference literature and dictionaries you need for the job.
- The opportunity to discuss translations and enjoy the interchange of ideas to the extent not normally possible if you work in isolation as a freelance.
- An opportunity to learn how to use the tools of the trade.

If you work with a large company you will have the opportunity of gaining experience and acquiring expertise in that particular company's industry. You will have access to experts in the relevant fields and probably a specialist library. If you are fortunate, you will be involved in all stages of documentation from translation, proof reading and checking through to desktop publishing. You will also be able to view your work long term.

If you work for a translation company, you will be exposed to a broader range of subjects but will not have the same close level of contact with experts. Your work may be restricted to checking and proof reading initially so that you can gain some feeling for the work before starting on translation proper. The smaller the company the more you will be exposed to activities that are peripheral to translation. This in itself can make the work more interesting and heighten your sense of involvement.

Your choice will be determined by what jobs are on offer and what your own skills and aspirations are. I would advise working for an industrial or commercial company first since working in a translation company often demands more maturity and experience than a newly-qualified translator can offer.

You may wonder how many words a translator is capable of producing in a day. Having worked together with and consulted other translation companies, the norm for a staff translator is around 1500 words a day or 33,000 a month. This may not seem a lot but there is more to translation than initially meets the eye. Individual freelance translators have claimed a translation output of 12,000 words in a single day without the use of computer-aided translation tools! The most I have completed, unaided, is just over 20,000 in three days. These are rates that are impossible to sustain because the work is so mentally draining that quality starts to suffer. Using a translation memory system I have been able to plough through 36,000 words in six working days. But, as you might surmise, this contained a high degree of repetition.

Working as a staff translator should provide a structured approach to the work and there should be a standard routine for processing the work according to the task in hand. Paperwork is a necessary evil or should I say a useful management tool and, if used properly, will make organisation of your work easier. Some form of record should follow the translation along its road to completion. This is considered in detail in Section 7.10 – Quality control operations.

1.10   Considering a job application

Any salary figures quoted in a book will, by their very nature, rapidly become outdated. Income surveys are carried out from time to time on rates and salaries by the ITI with results published in the *ITI Bulletin*. Present figures (2002) range from about £15,000 at the lower end to somewhere in the region of £25,000 for a translator/project manager.

As in any job, the salary you can command depends on your experience, expertise, any specialist knowledge you may have and, not least, your own negotiating powers. Results of surveys are published from time to time by the professional associations. Job adverts also give some indication of what salary is being offered.

When considering a position as a staff translator make sure that you get a written offer which encloses a job description to indicate your responsibilities, the opportunities for personal development and training, and a potential career path. Don't forget that you are also interviewing a potential employer to determine whether he can offer the type of work and career development that you are looking for. The following is an actual example of a job offer made to a fresh graduate without any professional experience. Though it is from 1997 it is still relevant.

Candidate   *May 27, 1997*
Street address
Town, County, Postcode

PRIVATE AND CONFIDENTIAL

Offer of employment – Staff translator and Checker

Dear (Candidate's Name),
As a result of discussions, and successful completion of two test translations under commercial conditions during your visit, I am pleased to offer you employment at our office in Bracknell. The principal terms of this offer are:

Position: *Staff translator and checker.*
Starting date: *Monday 1 September 1997. Actual date to be confirmed by mutual agreement.*
Working hours: *Full time. 35 hours per week. Core hours 9.00 to 17.00 with 60 minutes for lunch. Flexibility subject to approval.*
Holidays: *20 days per annum (pro rata for 1997) plus all public holidays.*

The probationary period applicable to new employees is three months. Thus your position will become permanent on 1 December 1997 subject to satisfactory completion of this period. The period of notice during this period is one week.
The following are your specific terms and conditions of service with Aardvark Translation Services Limited as of 1 September 1997 until further notice.

Position
You will be employed as a STAFF TRANSLATOR AND CHECKER.
Your principal duties are translation from Norwegian and Swedish into English, and checking other translators' translations. It is anticipated that your language skills will be extended to Danish with exposure to relevant texts.

Salary and benefits
Your salary as from 1 September 1997 will be £XX,000 per annum with the next scheduled salary review on 1 December 1997. Your salary will be paid monthly in arrears on or about the 23rd of each month. No sickness or injury benefits in addition to National Health provisions are provided at present.

(continued)

The company runs a non-contributory pension scheme in association with High Street Bank plc. You will be eligible for this benefit after 12 months' employment with the company. This will be in addition to statutory government provisions that are in operation. Time off will be allowed to attend medical or dental appointments on the understanding that some flexibility of hours worked is offered in return.

Proposed starting date
1 September 1997. Actual date to be confirmed by mutual agreement.

Working hours and holiday entitlement
Your normal working hours will be between 09.00 hrs and 17.00 hours with 60 minutes for lunch. Thus the total working hours per week are 35. Flexible hours are permitted providing these are agreed in advance.

Your initial holiday entitlement is 20 days paid holiday per calendar year plus all public holidays. If your employment does not span a full year, your entitlement will be calculated on a pro rata basis.

Responsible manager
Your responsible manager will be JA, Commercial Director. CL will act as your guardian angel – other translation staff can be consulted as appropriate. I will act as your guide and mentor where appropriate through One-to-One Consultations.

Training
Training will be carried out on the job and will be supplemented with in-house seminars on work-related tasks.

Notice of termination of employment
The period of notice of termination of employment to be given by ATS Limited to you is one calendar month. The period of notice of termination of employment to be given by you to ATS Limited is one calendar month.

Further education
Once you have completed one year of full-time service (31 August 1998), the company is prepared to consider sponsorship of further education that is pursued through a recognised educational establishment such as a local college or the Open University. This will form part of your structured career development.

(continued)

Sponsorship is subject to the discretion and approval of the Managing Director. Such further education shall be deemed to be of benefit to the company. The company will pay for the cost of the courses you wish to attend, plus the cost of the necessary books and course materials. Course books that are paid for by the company will remain the property of the company and shall be kept in the company's library once the course is completed.

If you discontinue your employment of your own volition while the course is in progress, or within one year of the course being completed, you will be obliged to reimburse the company to the full extent of the sponsorship of that course. This condition may be waived under special circumstances and at the discretion of the Managing Director.

Professional association fees will be reimbursed at the discretion of the company.

ACCEPTANCE OF TERMS AND CONDITIONS OF SERVICE

I hereby agree to and accept the above Terms and Conditions of Service.

Dated, ... August 1997.

. . . . .
(Candidate)

Please reply with your acceptance or rejection of this offer by Friday, 15 August 1997.

A non-disclosure form is also enclosed and requires your signature. We look forward to your joining the team.

Yours sincerely,

Managing Director
ATS Ltd.

Enc.   Staff Regulations
*   Non-disclosure agreement*

When discussing your employment, look at items that are general and not related specifically to the job of translator. These include:

- what induction procedure does the employer have?
- what do staff regulations cover?
- what career structure is in place?
- what personal and skills development is offered?

Don't forget that you are interviewing a potential employer as much as the employer is interviewing you.

1.11   Working as a freelance

Unrealistic expectations of freelance translators include:

- The ability to work more than 24 hours a day.
- No desire for holidays or weekends off.
- The ability to drop whatever you're doing at the moment to fit in a panic job that just has to be completed by this afternoon.
- The ability to survive without payment for long periods.
- . . .

No, that's not really true (unless you allow it to happen!). The essential attribute you *do* need is the discipline to structure your working hours. Try and treat freelance translation like any other job. Endeavour to work 'normal' office hours and switch on your answering machine outside these hours.

There are many temptations to lure the unwary (or perhaps I should say inexperienced) freelance. There could be unwarranted demands on your time by clients if you allow yourself to be talked into doing an assignment when, in all honesty, you should be enjoying some leisure time.

Plan your working hours to allow sufficient time to recover the mental energy you burn. There are of course times when you need to stretch your working hours. **Try not to make a habit of it**. If you become overtired it is all too easy to make a mistake.

There is the temptation to think that if you take a holiday, your client may go elsewhere. The answer to that is if your client values the quality of your work then he will come back to you after your holiday.

What you can expect to earn as a freelance translator depends on your capacity for work and the fees you can negotiate. Your net pre-tax income, to start with, will probably be in the region of £20,000. As you become more experienced, your production capacity will improve. Little differentiation is made in fees offered since translators are inevitable asked, 'How much do you charge per thousand words?' and that's about it. Certainly, little consideration is made of experience, evidence of specialist knowledge, continuous personal development since qualifying, or tangible evidence of quality management.

1.12 What's the difference between a translation company and a translation agency?

One decision you will need to make at one stage is whether to work for translation companies and agencies or whether to try and build up your own client base. There are advantages to both approaches.

It is perhaps worth giving a brief definition of translation companies and agencies. The former have their own in-house translators as well as using the services of freelances whereas the latter act purely as agencies, or translation brokers, and thereby rely solely on freelances. (I'll refer to translation companies and agencies collectively as 'agencies' for convenience since this is how clients perceive them). If you work for translation agencies you will be able to establish a good rapport. This will ensure a reasonably steady stream of work. You will also have the option of saying '*No thanks*' if you have no capacity at the time. It will also keep your administration to a low manageable level.

The fees offered by translation agencies will be lower than you can demand from direct clients. But consider the fact that agencies do all the work of marketing, advertising and selling to get the translation assignments. All you need do as a freelance, essentially, is to register with them and accept or reject the assignments offered. Working for translation agencies will also allow you to build up your expertise gradually.

Reputable translation agencies also make additional checks on the translations you submit. They may also spend a considerable amount of time reformatting a translation to suit a client's requirements. The fact that an agency performs these additional tasks does not in any way absolve you from producing the best possible translation you can for the intended purpose.

A word of caution

It is unethical to approach a translation agency's clients directly and attempt to sell them your services. You may consider it tempting but it is viewed as commercial piracy. (Remember all the legwork done by the agency in cultivating a client.) It will take you some time to establish a reputation as a translator. That reputation could be damaged irreparably if you attempt commercial piracy. The world of translators is quite small and word gets around incredibly quickly if you act unprofessionally.

1.13 Working directly with clients

If you decide to work with translation agencies, all you need to do is register with a number of them and hopefully you will receive a regular supply of work. The level of administration you will need to deal with will be quite small. You will need to advertise if you want to work directly with clients and this requires quite a different approach. There will be additional demands on your time that will swallow up productive and fee-earning capacity. Approaching potential clients directly requires a lot of work. The table below will perhaps allow you to make your own judgement.

Working with translation agencies	Working with direct clients
All major agencies advertise in the 'Yellow Pages' and are easily accessible.	How do you identify potential clients? How do you make yourself known?
A letter will usually suffice as an introduction after which you may be asked to complete an assessment form and carry out a test translation.	Who do you contact in a company? You may need to make a number of phone calls before you get to the right person. In fact, you may need to make around 100 phone calls before you can gain a single client.
If you produce a satisfactory test translation you will be listed as a freelance and, hopefully, will receive a regular supply of work that is appropriate for your individual skills.	You will be lucky to find a potential client that does not already have a supplier of translations. You also have to convince a potential client that you have something special to offer.
Most agencies pay at pre-arranged times. Make sure you negotiate acceptable terms of business!	Getting paid by some clients can take a long time. Make sure you have written agreement on terms of payment.
Holidays are 'allowed'.	What happens when you go on holiday?
You can decide which assignments you wish to accept from a translation agency.	It could be an inconvenience being at the beck and call of a client.

Table 1.   Choosing to work with agencies or direct clients

1.14   Test translations

Some people are a bit tetchy about doing a test translation. After all, you may argue that you have your degree – isn't that enough? Consider the small amount of time you may have to spend on a test translation – it's not very long. (Would you buy a computer or car without testing it first?) A test usually amounts to a page or so. I have however seen a case where a potential client has asked for a complete chapter from a book to be translated free of charge as a test! I often wonder if the client concerned has got the whole book translated free of charge by sending a different chapter to the required number of translators. Performing a test translation will give you a chance to shine and could be the start of a long-term working agreement.

Most clients demand that translation agencies provide test translations (often several in the same language using different translators). You can image the response from the potential client if the agency declined to provide samples. Consider the provision of test translations as a way of differentiating yourself from your competitors.

1.15 Recruitment competitions

Two major users of multilingual skills are the European Community and the United Nations. Both organisations employ a large number of multilingual service providers (translators, checkers, interpreters, lawyers, administrators, etc.).

1.15.1 The European Community

The qualifications required depend on the post for which the candidate intends applying. To give an indication of the qualifications required for the European Community, a Translator is required to have a full university degree or equivalent, two years' practical experience since graduating, a perfect command of the relevant mother tongue and a thorough knowledge of two other Community languages. An Assistant Translator is required to have obtained a full university degree within the last three years, a perfect command of the relevant mother tongue and a thorough knowledge of two other Community languages – no experience is required.

The European Community announces recruitment competitions for the following organisations:

- The Commission of the European Communities
- The Council of the European Union
- The European Parliament
- The Court of Justice
- The Court of Auditors
- The Economic and Social Committee

The information which follows pertains only to *written translation*.

For information about *interpreting* you need to apply to the Joint Interpreting and Conference Service.

The Commission's Translation Service consists of large subject-based departments, four in Brussels and two in Luxembourg, which specialise in translating documents relating to specific fields. Each department comprises eleven language units, one for each official language of the Union (the official languages of the European Union are

Danish, Dutch, English, Finnish, French, German, Greek, Italian, Portuguese, Spanish and Swedish). Each of these 66 units is led by a unit head.

Most European Union institutions recruit their translation staff through jointly organised open competitive examinations. The exceptions are the Court of Justice and the Council of the European Union, which, in view of their special requirements, hold their own competitions.

The competitions are held from time to time as vacancies arise for translators into a particular language. They are announced in a joint notice published in the Official Journal bearing a number in the series 'EUR/LA/ . . . ', and advertised simultaneously in the press of the language concerned. Competitions for English-language translators are advertised in the United Kingdom and in Ireland, and possibly in other countries. The most recent was published in September 2002 (ISSN 0378–6986).

The competition consists of written tests (multiple-choice questions and translations into English from two other official languages) and an oral test.

The competition procedure (from the deadline for applications through to the oral tests) takes eight to ten months on average. Successful candidates are placed on a reserve list.

To fill immediate vacancies, unit heads select entrants from the reserve list for further interviews and medical examinations. Those not called for interview, or called but not selected for appointment at this stage, may be recruited as vacancies arise until recruiting from that list closes. The period during which entrants are recruited from the reserve list may be extended.

The Commission's policy is to recruit at the starting grades, which for language staff means LA 8 (assistant translator) or LA 7 (translator).

General conditions of eligibility for competitions for translators or assistant translators

Nationality: candidates must be citizens of a Member State of the European Union.

Qualifications: candidates must hold a university or CNAA degree or equivalent qualification either in languages or in a specialised field (economics, law, science, etc).

Knowledge of languages: candidates must have perfect mastery of their mother tongue (own language) and a thorough knowledge of at least two other official European Union languages. Translators translate exclusively into their mother tongue.

Age: the upper age limits are 45 for LA 8 and LA 7 competitions.

Experience:

- No experience is required for LA 8 competitions, which are open only to candidates who obtained their degree no more than three years before the competition is announced.

A PRACTICAL GUIDE FOR TRANSLATORS

- At least three years' experience is required for LA 7 competitions. The experience may be in language work or in some relevant professional field (economics, finance, administration, law, science, etc.).

Practical information

Competitions for translators are normally held every three years for each language, although the interval is sometimes longer.

The Commission's 'Info-recruitment' office is open every weekday from 9.00 to 17.00, and will answer your questions on any aspect of recruitment to the European Union institutions.

Address: 34 rue Montoyer, B – 1000 Brussels
Telephone +32.2.299.31.31 – fax +32.2.295.74.88.

This information was accessed in September 2002. Check the European Union's website (http://europa.eu.int/comm/translation/en/recrut.html) for the latest information.

Tests comprise a written element and an oral element. Candidates are first obliged to take an elementary test that comprises a series of multiple choice questions to assess:

1. specialized knowledge of the field(s) covered by the competition and knowledge of the European Community and current affairs, particularly in Europe;
2. logical reasoning ability (numerical, symbolic and spatial, etc.);
3. knowledge of a second Community language (chosen by the candidate and specified on the application form).

The written tests vary according to the nature of duties. Candidates applying for work as a translator or interpreter must sit special language tests. Successful candidates then go through various selection stages for further assessment. Suitable candidates are then listed for approval by an appointing authority and may then be invited for a further interview with heads of department at the Commission or any other institution that may be interested in recruiting them. A definite job offer may be made after these interviews.

Information about forthcoming competitions can be found in the Official Journal of the European Communities. Write to the following address for more information:

INFO-RECRUITMENT
Recruitment Unit
Commission of the European Communities
rue de la Loi 200
B–1049 Brussels

1.15.2 The United Nations

A competitive examination for editors, translators/précis-writers and verbatim reporters takes place annually in order to establish a roster from which vacancies for editors, translators/précis-writers and verbatim reporters at United Nations Headquarters in New York, and at other duty stations (Geneva, Vienna, Nairobi, Beirut and Bangkok) are filled.

Applicants outside the Secretariat applying for the examination must:

- have the language that they are translating into as their main language;
- have a perfect command of English and an excellent knowledge of French and one of the other official languages of the United Nations (Arabic, Chinese, Russian and Spanish);
- hold a degree or qualification from a university or institution of equivalent status or hold a university degree from a school of translation.

On the basis of the results of this examination, selected candidates are invited for an interview. Candidates who are successful in this examination and are selected for inclusion in the roster are appointed to fill vacancies as they occur in the Editorial, Translation or Verbatim Reporting Services. When vacancies occur, successful candidates are recruited from the roster, subject to the requirements of the services in terms of expertise and language combinations. The assignments are subject to rotation, and successful candidates are sometimes called upon to serve at other duty stations in Africa, Asia, Europe, Latin America/Caribbean and Headquarters according to the needs of the Organisation. Successful candidates are expected to serve a minimum of five years in language posts. The selected candidates are normally offered an initial two-year probationary appointment at the P–2 level.

Contact information:

Examinations and Tests Section
Specialist Services Division
Office of Human Resources Management
Room *S–2575-E*
United Nations Secretariat
New York, N.Y. 10017
U.S.A
Fax: +1 212 963–3683

During my research, I have been in contact with government organisations that use translation services but generally these have not wished for their details to be published.

2 Bilingualism – the myths and the truth

'There are no foreign lands, only the traveller is foreign.'
Robert Louis Stevenson, 1850–1894

When I wrote this chapter for the first edition of the book in 1993, I telephoned the Institute of Translation and Interpreting with the intention of getting an accepted definition of bilingualism. I was informed politely that trying to get an answer would be as profitable as poking a stick into a hornet's nest.

If you have a copy of the Guinness Book of Records, look up the entry for the person who can supposedly 'speak' the most languages. When I wrote the first edition of this book, the entry read, 'In terms of oral fluency, the most multilingual living person is Derick Herning of Lerwick, Shetland, whose command of 22 languages earned him victory in the inaugural 'Polyglot of Europe' contest held in Brussels in May 1990'.

The Guardian newspaper published the obituary of Kenneth Hale, the linguist, on November 10, 2001. He was professor of Linguistics at the Massachusetts Institute of Technology and was said to be 'the master of more than 50 languages'.

The term bilingual is very much abused and the number of people who are truly bilingual is very small. You may have seen job advertisements for a 'Bilingual Secretary'. I suppose the argument is that a person who is that well qualified would not be working as a secretary. (This is no reflection on the abilities of a good secretary).

The number of people who are listed in the Institute of Translation and Interpreting Directory as being competent to work into more than one language is very small. There is a term called 'language of habitual use'. You may have learned one language as a child and then moved to a different country. The language of that country will probably become your language of habitual use. There is also the term 'main language' in use in the European Community.

The ITI demands evidence of any claim to be bilingual before the person concerned can be listed as having this qualification. The 'main language' would be the natural choice for listing in the directory. Assessment of any claim for an additional language is done by taking an examination or submitting written evidence in support of the claim.

Just as a matter of interest, look at the following graph (Ref. 3) which illustrates the

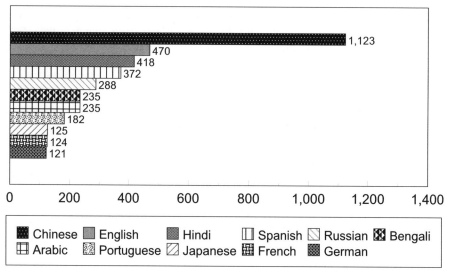

Chinese	1,123
English	470
Hindi	418
Spanish	372
Russian	288
Bengali	235
Arabic	235
Portuguese	182
Japanese	125
French	124
German	121

0   200   400   600   800   1,000   1,200   1,400

■ Chinese ■ English ■ Hindi ⊞ Spanish ⧄ Russian ▨ Bengali
⊞ Arabic ▨ Portuguese ⧄ Japanese ▦ French ■ German

Figure 2. World's major languages

number of people (in millions) who speak the world's major languages, either as their first language or second (working) language.

Certainly in the Western World, it would appear that English (in its various guises) is the *lingua franca*. Statistics indicate that as a result of Sweden, Finland and others joining the European Union, English is the most widely used language in the EU. This is confirmed by a report in the Financial Times (Ref. 4) that quotes an unpublished survey of more than 1 billion document pages translated at the European Commission. This states that 42 percent were translated from English compared with 40 percent from French.

The Institute of Linguists publishes a booklet entitled 'Bilingual Skills Certificate and Certificate in Community Interpreting'. It offers the following definitions on bilingualism:

Bilingual service providers are people who possess two sets of skills – language and professional skills, so that they can give the same standard of service in the context of two languages and cultures. In order to provide an equal standard of service to all clients, the people providing the service should have adequate standards of training and qualifications in both sets of skills. For example, allowing people to give medical advice or gather information upon which medical decisions are made when they are not qualified and solely on the grounds that they happen to speak French or Urdu is as bad as giving good medical advice which cannot be understood.

Total bilingualism or ambilingualism means having an equal or complete functional competence in two languages, which involves an equal understanding of both cultures.

Bilingualism is usually described as using two languages in daily life – but not necessarily in the same context. Therefore, one can be bilingual but not have a command of both languages in the same subject area.

Bilingual service providers should have an adequate competence in both languages and an objective understanding of the implications concerning both cultures in the subject area in which they work.

Being bilingual does not necessarily include the ability to interpret or translate. This requires additional skills in order to transfer concepts between languages.

I have used Swedish as a working language for more than 30 years and have translated the language for almost that length of time. I speak the language almost every day and spend weeks at a time working in Sweden. Yet I would shy clear of submitting a translation into Swedish unless it were to be used purely for information purposes. Yes, you may be able to translate quite correctly into a foreign language but it will eventually become evident that the translation was not written by a 'native'. The only way to get around this is to get the text checked by a 'native' but this is usually an unsatisfactory compromise.

Probably the least satisfactory task is 'laundering' a text produced by a non-native speaker and given to you with the bland statement, 'I've already translated this, will you please have a quick look at it just to check the English'. More often than not, it is quicker to translate the piece afresh. The person submitting the request is under the illusion that he is saving money in this way. He will no doubt have spent some considerable time on producing the draft and it is difficult to tell the person concerned that the time may have been less than productive. An example is given in the Appendix. You can, of course, learn something from the terminology used in some cases. If I do not feel happy about accepting a 'laundering' assignment I will politely decline the offer and explain the reasons why.

On the following page is an example of such a text written by a Swede. It took the best part of an hour to try and make sense of what was written whereas a clean translation from Swedish into English would have taken half the time. *** are used to disguise the guilty.

There are times when your diplomacy will be tested since there are people who, having a knowledge of a foreign language, will question your use of that language. Let's assume for the sake of example that this is English. Such people come in a number of categories:

- Those who have a basic knowledge of English and who wish merely to criticise either to demonstrate their knowledge or just for the sake of it. I have seen many cases where people have 'corrected' a translation and have introduced errors. To these people all you can do is point out the error(s) and perhaps explain what would be the consequence of retaining it (them).
- Those whose style differs from yours. If this style is more appropriate then accept it.

********* HOLIDAY   *Version Europe*

The Christmas catalog will give your customers ideas for Christmas gifts! The consumer will find inspiration and new ideas.

CHRISTMAS WISHES!

You can reach your customers directly! Use your stores register of addresses for direct mailing! You will find the name of your store in the catalog. How many cataloges do you need? We need you order at latest the 15th of October.

HOLIDAY ADVERTISING

********* will make a double spread in important interior magazins. How do you do your local advertising for Christmas? ********* will as usual do ready made advertising material for that, both in color and in black and white. Please, contact ********* for material.

CHRISTMAS DECORATION CARD

To each member of the Marketing program 2002, we will send instore material to give extra attention to ********* in your store.

After all, the client should know his business and you should be receptive to constructive comments.

- Those who can offer constructive comments in terms of terminology – again, here is an opportunity to enhance your expertise.

The letter on the next page is not untypical. It was sent to a large number of potential clients in the UK from an estate agent in Sweden with the aim of attracting interest in a property just north of Stockholm. Only the names have been removed to protect the guilty.

I later heard a comment from a cynic who reckoned that the letter was written in this way to guarantee that it would be the centre of discussion! Be philosophical – you can always learn from the mistakes of others.

2.1   Target language and source language

These are convenient terms and are really self-explanatory. The source language is the language you are working from whereas the target language is the language you are working into (your language of habitual use). Most people charge according to the number of words in the source language since this is what is supplied by the client. There has been, and will continue to be, heated discussion on which is the most appropriate method but this book is not the forum for this discussion. How to charge for your work is discussed in Chapter 4.

1991. 4 September

Dear Sirs,

Concerning the project (. . .) Sweden.

We take the liberty of sending You some information about the above headline. The (. . .) is a very representative . . . building and under up construktion and it will be ready to move into 1992, the First of Feb.

The property is in a very rigth place, about 70 kilometres from Stockholm the capital of Sweden and to Arlanda, the international and domestic airport is it only 20 minutes drive, without any queues, that is a save of time!!! Into Uppsala city, down town, is it about 5 minutes drive and the buscommunications traffics here very frequntly.

The (. . .) is built in a very venturesome architecture, with the daylight coming through the roof and there is an atrium, with lots of trees and flowers surrounded by mirrors of water. The environment feels very important to day for a pleasant and nice workingenvironment.

We will appreciate, if unprejudiced, through a meeting get us the honour to present You more deeper and detailed information and this objects possibilitys.

This purpose is given to attract Yours intrests for a possibly renting. We would like to see you here in Sweden for a businesslunch, with a following showing of the building, this unique project as it says.

Yours sincerely,

2.2   Target language deprivation

There is a risk of becoming linguistically schizophrenic. Because your brain is so fluent in both languages, it is fooled into thinking that the structure you have put together in the target language is correct merely because it is correct in the source language.

Target language deprivation is one of the problems experienced by translators working in their adopted country. They become so totally immersed in the language and culture that they lose their linguistic edge – they begin to think like a native. I know in my own case that it took me at least six months to speak proper English again after having lived in Sweden for 10 years. This was despite reading or at least glancing through an English language newspaper and magazines most days.

2.3   Retaining a sharp tongue

To understand a language properly and to translate it successfully you must keep up with cultural change. This is why the best translations are made by a native speaker who is resident in the country where the target language is spoken. A language undergoes continuous change and development – sometimes to its detriment, unfortunately. (I was chided with the statement, *'That's very old school'* for having this attitude – but that is my opinion. I'm homeostatic and sometimes resent change.). The best of both worlds, of course, is being able to travel to the source language country to work on assignments. This allows you to retain the sharp edge of your mother tongue while keeping up to date with the source language and culture.

Our Father, who art in heaven, Hallowed be thy Name. Thy kingdom come; Thy will be done; In earth as it is in heaven. Give us this day our daily bread. And forgive us our trespasses. As we forgive them that trespass against us. And lead us not into temptation; But deliver us from evil: For thine is the Kingdom, The power; and the glory, For ever and ever. *Amen.*	Our Father in heaven, hallowed be your name, your kingdom come, your will be done, on earth as in heaven. Give us today our daily bread. Forgive us our sins as we forgive those who sin against us. Lead us not into temptation but deliver us from evil. For the kingdom, the power, and the glory are yours now and for ever. *Amen.*

I have seen significant changes in my own lifetime. Some I am happy to accept whereas others make the English language poorer by their introduction. The following example shows the differences in the Lord's Prayer taught by the Church of England. The version to the left is the one I learned as a child whereas the version to the right is the one used in my local church. I must say that I prefer the use of the second person singular in this context.

There are, of course, many versions and translations and research on the Internet produces interesting linguistic challenges. Microsoft Word's spell checker rejects 'thine' but not 'Thy' since the latter is capitalised.

2.4   Localisation

This is a relatively new term but illustrates the importance of the command of the target language. If a translation is to be used in published form, such as a catalogue or manual, a serious client will send your translation to his counterpart in the country where the translated document can be checked to ensure that

- it is suitable for the intended market,
- terminology reflects what is in current use, and
- the language used is pitched at the right level.

This is no reflection on your ability as a translator but an endeavour to ensure that the language used is topical and relevant for the intended market. There is a downside to this on occasions since the foreign subsidiary may view this as an opportunity to edit your translation or heavily criticise it. This is particularly the case if the subsidiary felt that it should have been given the job of translation.

It is surprising how many translations are used directly without any pretence of quality control by the client. The original language document will probably have undergone several revisions before final approval. The translator usually has but one stab at the work. I suppose the argument is that the text you are given to translate is in its final, approved form and all you need to do is to put it into a different language. This is a prime case for trying to 'educate' or at least make the client aware of what the translation process entails.

A client would not dream of printing a brochure in the source language without first checking at least one proof. Several equally-valid versions may have been considered before the final version of the source text was approved. While not advocating that several different translations should be considered, a proper level of suitability assessment should be applied to the translated document.

The essential factor to consider is the target reader. This governs choice of language, presentation, the level at which the language is aimed etc. A manual may be written in English and intended for use by mechanics or technicians in a developing country. English is used merely as a working language and, as a consequence, the language needs to be elementary but not patronisingly simple. This requires skills in what is termed 'Simplified English'.

When working as a technical editor at Volvo in Sweden, I paid a visit to a UK rival's technical documentation centre. At that time, the company concerned produced several 'English' language versions of their car owner's manuals: North American, European, South African, Australasian and English for the Indian sub-continent! This is perhaps an extreme example but it does show that the language does need to be suited to or localised for the intended reader.

The advent of satellites, electronic mail and instant access have led to the development of news networks such as CNN. CNN is now available worldwide in most large hotels and, with similar networks originating from the USA, is often the principal source of English language news. This source is ethnocentric since it reports news from a US perspective and, as such, is how a lot of people learn English. One could also argue that this is cultural imperialism but that hypothesis is politically-loaded. I would contend that the English spoken in the US has now diverged so much from 'British' English that it ought to be classified as a separate language. What it should be called is a hard choice since 'American' would no doubt upset the Hispanic population of the USA.

For those who wish to read more on the development of English as a world language I recommend Bill Bryson's books '*Mother Tongue*' and '*Made in America*'.

2.5   Culture shocks

I remember a particular occasion when I was a university student in Sweden. I had been living in the country for over three years. I would like to think that my knowledge of Swedish was reasonable since I had already taken the qualifying examination, in Swedish, for university entrance (*studentexamen*). I was in my second year at university studying physics after having already read a year of mathematics. To supplement my student grant I worked as a night porter at a hotel. Among other things, this work involved manning the telephone switchboard and reception desk at night. On Saturdays the hotel had dinner-dances and the last guests usually left at around midnight. I locked up at about half-past midnight and settled down studying my physics notes. The resident chef had finished in the kitchen and was out walking his dog prior to retiring for the night.

While deep in thought about the quantum theory of electrical conductivity I was disturbed by a guest from the dinner-dance who staggered down the stairs to reception. He asked for a toilet and, rather than making him go back up the stairs again, I offered him the facility of using the staff toilet adjacent to reception. He reappeared some while later with glass in hand and pronounced, 'Staff have been drinking on duty, I shall report this to the health authorities!'. I hypothesised mentally for a brief moment and explained that I had not seen a glass the last time I checked the toilet during a security walkabout. He detected that I spoke Swedish with a foreign accent and made the obvious but inebriated remark, '*So you're a foreigner are you? You must be one of these bloody refugees that come here to live off the state!*' This was followed by an enquiry as to my nationality and, when he found out that I was English, he demanded the use of a telephone. He explained that his son had been to England on holiday and would have to come to the hotel to act as an interpreter. The fact that we had been conversing successfully so far in Swedish seemed to have escaped him. His son refused to come to the hotel and there followed an uncomfortable period while I endeavoured to placate the less than sober guest.

Fortunately, the chef returned after walking his dog – a large Alsatian. The chef had met this troublesome guest before and suggested that he either go home or stay overnight in the hotel. The guest's wife refused to collect him at such a late hour and he declined to take a taxi. The upshot was that he was shown a room at the hotel and retired for the night. Thank goodness for resident chefs with Alsatians! The guest's wife came and bailed him out in the morning. Unfortunately for him, the only vacant room left just happened to be the most expensive. As a result of discussion with the hotel manager later on, the guest was banned from the hotel since this was not the first time he has made life uncomfortable for hotel staff.

There is the argument, of course, that this was not so much a culture shock as being the victim of drunken chauvinism.

The figure on the following page illustrates the cycle of expatriation and repatriation plus the attendant culture shocks. The latter occur not only when you move to a country but also when you move back to your country of origin.

2.6   Stereotypes

In no country will there be universal agreement about ideas that underlie that country's culture. There will be people who hold cultural values quite strongly and those who hold them not at all. The attribution of cultural traits to individuals from a given culture is called 'stereotyping'. The word has negative connotations but you should be aware that stereotyping is not necessarily bad. In fact, it is a natural consequence of the ways in which we communicate.

Reference to books on culture and stereotyping are given in the reading list at the end of this book.

It is important to note the following about stereotypes:

- Stereotypes are automatic, and cannot be avoided. They are the ways in which we organise our thinking in new situations.
- Stereotypes are derived from experience with members of other groups or from secondary sources. In either case, they arise because we have too little accurate information to go on.
- Stereotypes can be moved closer to reality by increased contact with the group that is being stereotyped.
- If the stereotyper's perception of another group is positive or neutral, the stereotype will believe (wrongly) that the other group is 'just like us'.
- Stereotypes, in and of themselves, do not lead to miscommunication. The problems arise if they are inaccurate and are held too rigidly. The predictions made by them will be wrong, and this will lead to misunderstanding.
- If we want to communicate effectively with strangers, we should not seek to avoid stereotypes. What we need to do is to increase the complexity and accuracy of our stereotypes. We can do this by constantly questioning them.

Language reflects culture and the translator must understand cultural and stereotypical ways to reproduce the meaning of the source text. Good examples are business letters where a letter written by a French person would appear very polite whereas a letter written by a German person might appear blunt and almost rude. In these cases, the

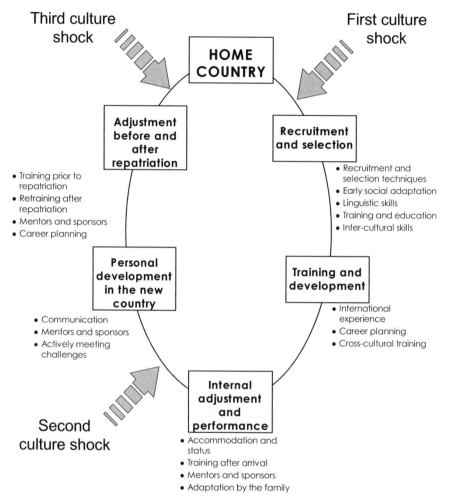

Figure 3. Expatriation and repatriation, and the attendant culture shocks

English translator must adapt the letter so that the English reader will react in the same way to the letter as would a French or German reader.

One of the dilemmas of being totally fluent in a second language is which cultural affiliation to adopt. My philosophy is to adopt the one that is most beneficial in the circumstances at the time.

3 The client's viewpoint

'Arguments out of a pretty mouth are unanswerable'
Joseph Addison, 1672–1719

One of the purposes of translation is to add value to an original document as well as facilitating communication and comprehension. Since a company's documentation is often the only tangible evidence that it exists, any translation must be of the same high quality as the original. The quality of the original may not always be high and often the translation is of a better quality but more of this later.

Consider your reaction when you receive a document from a foreign client. It is likely that you will pay far more attention to it if the document is in a language that you comprehend. The same applies when you send documentation to a client – it is far more likely to be favourably received if it is professionally translated into the client's language.

3.1 Who should you get to translate?

The principal criteria applied to the selection of a translator are:

1. use only a translator who translates into his mother tongue (or language of habitual use as it is sometimes called). Ideally, the translator should have formal training as a translator and be qualified as a Member of a recognised professional association such as the Institute of Translation and Interpreting.
2. use only a translator who has experience of your product or service segment. It is inappropriate to ask a translator with experience of, say, only electronic engineering to translate a text on property management.

To do otherwise is unprofessional and unethical.

The Institute of Translation and Interpreting has produced a guide to buying translations written by Chris Durban and designed by Antonio Aparacio entitled '*Translation – getting it right*'. This handy booklet is available from the ITI or as a .pdf file on its website (www/iti.org).

3.2   The service provider and the uninformed buyer

The term 'seller' is a misnomer since translations cannot be sold from stock. Although I think that many buyers often believe that this is the case. As I wrote in the introductory chapter, some potential buyers are woefully ill-informed of the skills needed for translation. Here is the opportunity to do some effective marketing. The buyer has some idea of what he wants and it is up to you to advise him of what is involved and what the realistic costs are. The following lists some of the false ideas and how you should advise, or dare I say, educate the buyer.

CLIENT MISCONCEPTION	REALITY
A translator works on his own and needs no support from the client.	Dialogue between translator and client is essential since, even though the translator should have experience in the client's subject area, there will be times when clarification on poorly-written or ambiguous text will be necessary or advice on terminology will be sought
A translated text of, say, 5000 words can be produced overnight and costs no more than £20.	A qualified translator is a highly skilled professional and is no less equal in stature to other professions that demand a similar level of education and experience.
The client has already attempted a translation, or may have asked a member of staff to do so. The client then requests that you 'just have a look at the text and tidy it up'.	You should reject a request of this type and inform the client that the result would be a poor compromise and would probably cost as much, if not more, to 'tidy' up than it would to make a new translation.
If you have a computer, it can do the translation for you and your charges should be lower.	Translation tools such as computer-aided translation need the skills of an experienced translator to interact with the computer to produce a professional result. The client is paying for your skills as a 'knowledge worker' and for the end result. Make the client aware of the benefits you are offering. Would the client demand that a solicitor charge less because he uses the same efficiency tools such as word-processing software, databases?
The client makes the bold statement, 'I only need a rough translation, you needn't spend too much time on it'.	We as professionals do not produce 'rough translations'. You need to explain to the client that you will produce an accurate translation but that the level of quality control will mean that the output is suitable for information purposes but not for general publication. (See Chapter 7, Quality control and accountability)

Table 2.   Common client misconceptions and reality

You may know these truths to be self-evident but need to ensure that the potential client understands that translation is a skilled and demanding profession.

Some international companies may have their own staff translators either in-house or at their various international subsidiaries. This is ideal if the people concerned have the appropriate training and experience, and translate into their mother tongue. If it is not cost-effective to retain such resources then the obvious step is to establish a beneficial working relationship with an external resource.

There is a variety of external resources available but the challenge is how to select the best translation services provider for your particular needs. This choice is particularly difficult if you do not have the staff to assess the quality of the translations provided – you have to rely on the integrity of the service provider.

3.3   How to find a translation services provider

If you look in the section for Translators and Interpreters in the London Business Pages, for example, you will find literally hundreds of firms from 'one-man bands' to translation companies with a significant number of permanent staff. Faced with this dilemma, it is difficult to know whom to choose. If you really want to play it safe, ask a translation service provider if its quality management system is accredited to ISO 9001. The proportion of translation services providers who are accredited to this standard (ISO 9001: 2000 – previously 9002:1994) and others such as 'Investors in People' is quite small. However, on this basis you may wish to extend your search a little.

There are agencies who, in their advertising, make the bold statement 'ISO 9002 applied for'. This implies no qualification whatsoever. An organisation is either accredited or it is not accredited. Regrettably the potential buyer may not be aware of this.

Most advertisers offer much the same in terms of the range of services, speedy delivery, and number of languages. Very few offer differentiated services and the statement 'all languages, all subjects' often belies the actual resources available. There are three principal types of translation service provider.

The individual freelance translator or practitioner working from one or more languages and into one target language. This may be the best option if you need translation into a single language. It is natural that the individual practitioner will have limited resources but, if you can work within these limitations, then your requirements can be met. Refer to Table 3 below.

Translations agencies who, as the name suggests, act as an agency or broker. These are sometimes staffed by as few as two or three administrators. There are good and bad agencies. If you are an uninitiated buyer of translation services it is useful to have a list of questions to ask when asking for details. Again, refer to Table 3.

Services provided	Types of translation services provider			
	Freelance translator	Small translation agency	Non-accredited medium-sized translation agency	Accredited translation company
Range of languages	Limited	Limited	Yes	Yes
Range of hardware and software	Limited	Limited	Yes	Yes
In-house translation resources	Yes	No	No	Yes
External translation resources	No	Yes	Yes	Yes
Independent checking	No	No	Possibly	Yes
Glossary compilation	Yes	No	Limited	Yes
Project management	Limited	Limited	Yes	Yes
Reference library	Limited	Limited	Limited	Yes
Translation tools	Limited	No	No	Yes
Desk top publishing facilities	Limited	Limited	Possibly	Yes
Software localisation and verification	Limited	No	No	Yes
Website translation	Limited	Limited	Limited	Yes
Capacity to handle major projects in several languages	No	Limited	Yes	Yes
Accreditation to ISO 9001:2000	Very few	Very few	No	Yes

Table 3.   Matrix of services provider options

Translation companies have their own in-house translators and quality controllers who work under what might be considered ideal conditions. Staff translators can discuss linguistic challenges with colleagues and have a greater advantage in this respect over individual practitioners. Many of the latter work in isolation – one of the dilemmas of working as a freelance. Those who shun isolation and network with colleagues are at an advantage.

3.4   Is price any guide to quality?

Good quality translation takes time and costs money. All buyers of translation services will want value for money but this does not necessarily mean that the cheapest is the least expensive in the long term. Many translation services providers will quote a low price for translation, just to get a 'foot in the door', but will then add supplements for additional services such as:

- 'technical translation'
- independent checking
- layout
- project management
- glossary compilation.

It is therefore important to ask what is included in the price. It is also important to ask what the translation services provider's quality policy is and request a copy of it. This will give a good indication whether or not the translation services provider is serious about quality management or is just paying lip service to the concept.

A reliable method is to use a translation services provider who is recommended by a colleague or associate. Again the caveat is whether or not the colleague is able to assess the quality provided. Translation is but one element of the documentation value chain so it is important that the source document be suitable for the intended reader. A translation services provider has great difficulty making 'a silk purse out of a sow's ear'.

The following presents a number of options when seeking a services provider. Although 'No' is written in some cases, such services or attribute may not be appropriate to the individual translator. ISO 9001:2000 is a case in point.

3.4.1   What happens to an assignment when it goes to a translator

Though the translation process should be transparent to the client, it is important to know what happens to it once the client has handed it over to the translator. I have used the generic term translator in this context since the flowchart shown on the next page illustrates how a translation is handled from the time it leaves the client to when it is delivered. This process is taken from the ISO 9001 documentation of a translation company.

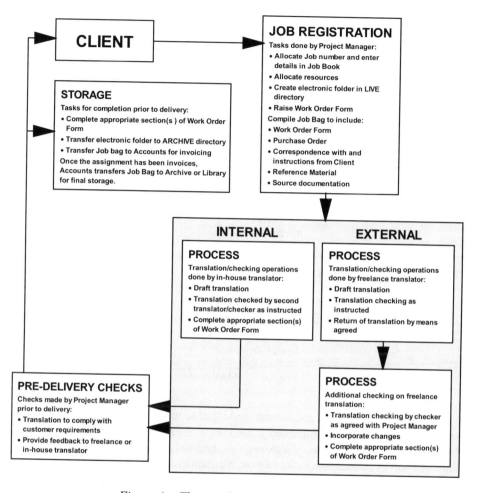

Figure 4. The translation handling process

3.5 Communication with the translation services provider

One of the principal uses for translations is to facilitate communication. It is therefore important that there be clear and unambiguous communication with the translation services provider at all times during the translation process. Quality gaps can arise at any stage if communication is not clear. This is illustrated in the following (Ref. 5).

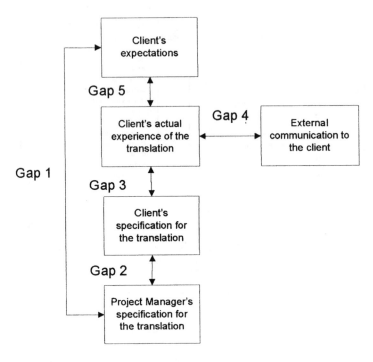

Figure 5.   Quality gaps

A good example of how a statement could lead to misinterpretation is, *'I'll blow up the fax and send it in bits!'*. Admittedly, this is a statement taken out of context and could be expressed more clearly as, *'I'll enlarge the original fax pages and send each as two enlarged halves'*, rather than a statement of intention to destroy the fax machine and send the pieces. I was once asked to define what 'communication' is. This can be any number of things but, in translation, I consider the following to be appropriate.

> The essence of communication is clarity of expression and correct understanding of the message.
>
> Communicate in the right language and people will understand.

The different gaps and their significance are shown in the following table.

Quality gap	How the quality gap arises
Gap 1 – the gap between what the client expects and the project manager's understanding of what the client wants	The gap arises when the project manager does not understand what the client considers to be important to the translation process. The client may expect a perfectly-formatted, independently-checked and edited translation (although has not specifically stated so) whereas the project manager believes that the translation will be used for information purposes only and requires no special layout.
Gap 2 – the gap between the project manager's perception of what the client wants and the actual specification for the translation	The gap arises when the project manager does not draw up a specification that is detailed enough to show clearly what is required. This may leave the translator who actually carries out the translation unsure about what exactly is intended. The gap may be a consequence of the translation requirements not being stated adequately by the client. For example, the client may expect the translation to be provided in a particular software format whereas the translator is not informed of this.
Gap 3 – the gap between the client specification and how the client views what is delivered	This gap arises when the delivered translation does not correspond to what was specified by the client. One example is the translation being longer than expected. It is the client's perception that is important but there may be a number of intangible factors that were not anticipated.
Gap 4 – the gap between the client's experience and external communication to the client.	This arises when the translation provider cannot deliver what is promised in advertising or promotion material. In other words, the translation provider must make sure that what is promised is, in fact, delivered.
Gap 5 – the gap between the client's expectation and the client's experience	A client's expectation is affected by his own experiences, the recommendations of others and the claims made by the translation services provider. The translation services provider must bear in mind that the client's experience is determined by his perception of what is supplied, not by the perception held by the translation services provider.

Table 4.   Quality gaps that can arise in translation

4 Running a translation business

'Creditors have better memories than debtors.'
Benjamin Franklin, 1706–1790

4.1 Starting a business

I would like to quote the Open Business School (part of the Open University), '*Running a business can be a dangerous activity for yourself and for others – just ask any of the 170,000 businesses that cease trading each year. In fact it is estimated that one in three businesses cease trading within their first three years of life – and two in three within their first ten years. And yet, although you need a licence to drive a car or fly a plane, you need nothing but reckless nerve and a first client to start a business.*'

Make sure you understand the implications and responsibilities of running a business before you commit yourself. The business world can be very harsh and can show very little sympathy. Make sure that you have written terms and conditions of doing business that you can apply. However, it is not enough to make a unilateral declaration of your terms and conditions. They have to be accepted in writing by your client to be valid.

Quite often, a client will attempt to impose his terms. The important consideration is to work to a mutually-agreed set of terms. Then, if a delay in payment occurs, you will at least have this as a basis for voicing your concern. More on this, however, in Chapter 9 What to do if things go wrong.

The simplest type of business is operating as a 'sole proprietor'. This incurs the least amount of administration and fewest legal formalities. There are many books readily available to advise and which contain far more useful information than I am able to offer. Local technical colleges often run short courses for people starting out in business. The courses are usually held in the evenings and cover topics such as taxation for small businesses, basic book keeping and accounting, and marketing.

4.2 Is translation a financially-rewarding career?

The answer to this question depends on your aspirations and what rewards are offered by other careers that you might be considering.

The translation profession comprises mostly freelances who, for the most part, work on their own and have little day-to-day contact with fellow practitioners. A large number of freelances work for translation companies.

This is one of the greatest limitations of the profession in terms of financial rewards since there is no coherent fee structure recommendation as, for example, in the case of solicitors. Furthermore there is little differentiation between the fees paid to newly-qualified translators and those with years of experience and a record of continuous personal development.

If you go through university and gain an MA or Diploma in Translation you will have spent at least four years as a student by the time you qualify. You will have incurred a debt of around £7000 for tuition fees unless you are fortunate to get a grant or have parents who can support you financially. In addition you need to pay for books, course material, food, accommodation and a host of other things while you are a student. It is not unrealistic to suggest that it costs you around £20,000 to become an academi-cally-qualified translator.

According to the 'Guideline hourly rates (charging rates) for solicitors 2001', fees for various legal professionals in GBP in the United Kingdom are as follows:

	London	Lowest outside London (Leicester)
Solicitors with over 8 year's experience	328	130
Solicitors with over 4 years' experience and under 8 years' experience	235	125
Other solicitors, legal executives and other fee earners	180	100
Trainee solicitors, paralegals and other fee earners	110	78

Translators are usually paid per 1000 words irrespective of the time taken. Let's assume an average rate of GBP 65 per 1000 words offered by translation companies to freelances. The productive working rate that even an experience translator can achieved (including research, proof reading, correction and editing) is somewhere around 320 words an hour. This equates to around GBP 21 an hour!

I know from experience that, on average, I can work productively for 6 hours a day although there are days when I work a lot longer (and, conversely, days when I am less productive). I have also keyed in draft translation work at a rate of 1100 words an hour. But this is exceptional. Let's assume that you work for 46 weeks of the year if you count annual holidays and public holidays, and the time you spend on continuous personal development in one form or another.

If you work this out on an annual basis your turnover is likely to be in the region of GBP 32,000. This sounds quite reasonable but then you need to consider the cost of running your business.

The following is a simple profit and loss statement. It assumes that you have registered a limited company and are working on your own from home and gives an indication of what your income and expenditure could look like:

Translation fees		32000
Salary, PAYE, NI	24000	
Gross profit		8000
Fixed costs		
Advertising and promotion	1000	
Professional fees (accounts, PAYE, etc.)	1000	
Travel	500	
Postage and stationery	100	
Telecommunications	1200	
Newspapers and books	400	
Computer hardware & software	500	
Accounts and payroll charges	1000	
Consultancy and professional fees	500	
Training	300	
Repairs and renewals	200	
Bank charges and interest	250	
Subscriptions	300	
Insurance	450	
Total	7200	
Pre-tax profit		300

This indicates that your monthly 'salary' after tax is around GBP 1300 depending on your personal circumstances. The figure for pre-tax profit is somewhat misleading since there are items such as depreciation, tax-allowable expenses (costs) to be considered. It is however useful as a guide. Bank charges and interest are included since, if you do work for translation companies outside the country where you are working, you will incur fees from your bank for negotiating foreign payments.

The most recent survey conducted by the ITI in 2001 noted that 40% of the respondents earned less than GBP 15,000 a year. The survey also states '*The average hourly rate of GBP 24.61 for translation companies is less than that of most skilled tradesmen while a significant number of respondents charge the same rates as secretarial services*'.

What you need to consider is whether or not you think the fees you can charge are reasonable recompense for the years of study and the debts you have incurred. You have several choices:

1. Consider some other profession
2. Accept the relatively low fees that are on offer
3. Negotiate more acceptable fees that are appropriate to your education, qualifications and experience.

Not until translators decline to accept work that pays low rates will there be any change. Some while back a translation company recently sent the following email to its freelances.

Dear Translator,

I am writing from XXXXX (also known as YYYYY Ltd) and as you know, you are registered on our database as a freelance translator.

XXXXX, one of Europe's largest Language Management companies, has been chosen by over half of the FTSE 100 for translations between 115 languages. This is due to exceptional responsiveness and quality. We continue to grow our business and secure major new contracts with some of the largest companies in the world.

However, the market for translation is tightening and we are experiencing real pressure on our prices, experiencing reductions in the region of 15%. Customers are negotiating very hard before placing work with us and we believe this situation is not just for XXXXX but is industry-wide. In order to ensure our continued competitiveness we are expecting you to reduce your prices also.

We hold our translators in the highest regard and recognise their immense contribution to the success of XXXXX. We would like to carry on the good working relationship already existing between XXXXX and its suppliers. We will only be able to do so if our suppliers (this means you) accept to reduce their rates.

As from ZZZZ 1st 2002, with immediate effect, we expect our translation suppliers to reduce their rates significantly. As you know XXXXX is regarded as highly professional and pay their suppliers on time. I hope that you will continue to be part of XXXXX and I look forward to our future relationship.

Thanking you for you [*sic*] interest in XXXXX .

If initiatives such as this are accepted then translators will continue to be highly-qualified but poorly-paid professionals. Anybody considering studying to become a translator may decide that the potential rewards are not attractive and will decide on some other profession.

There is a mutual dependence between translation companies and freelance translators. Translation companies also have a duty to educate clients and engender an understanding of the skills, tools and experience required to produce good quality translation. Similarly, professional organisations such as the Institute of Translation and Interpreting have role to play in enhancing the status of the profession and publishing guidelines, like the one quote above for solicitors, to ensure acceptable fees are paid.

There was the view just a few years ago, especially among non-translators, that advances in technology would quickly make the job of the translator redundant. This would be achieved as follows:

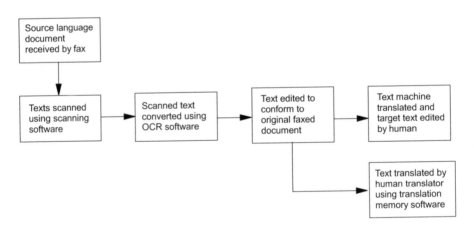

Figure 6. Idealistic view of translation without the translator

I'm happy to say that affordable scanners still require the result of text scanning to be heavily edited (especially if the layout is complex) and, as yet, the above process is still some way off being a fully practical and cost-effective option.

4.3 Support offered to new businesses

A number of enterprises offer support for new businesses. Knowing where to get information on such support can soften the burden of starting a business both in terms of advice and financial assistance through grants and subsidised schemes.

The Department of Trade and Industry offers support and advice through the Small Business Enterprise Scheme or Small Firms Advice Service. This will in all probability be operated through a local Business Link or firm of consultants.

Your bank will have an advisory service for small businesses. Seek the advice of this service since the scope of the public and private schemes that are available does change.

4.4 Counting words

The most common method applied for charging (at least in the United Kingdom) is per thousand words – usually source rather than target words. It is ideal if the client can specify the number and, if you consider the count to be correct, there need be no discussion of what is to be charged.

You will gradually develop a feel for how many words you can complete in an hour. Thus if you produce, say, 600 words an hour in draft form, a job that takes 4 hours to type should be around 2400 words long. This is providing you have not had to spend time on figures and layout.

There is always the thorny question of numerical data in a translation, particularly in financial reports. If you have to retype sets of figures the usual maxim is to count three blocks of figures (e.g. £7,600 £5,623 £1,893) as one word for the purpose of charging. Figures are more difficult to type and check than words. The client may not need the figures retyped and may be satisfied with the relevant headings and captions being typed and annotated. Ask about this when preparing a quotation.

There is always disparity between the number of source words and target words. Up to 30% in some cases depending on your own style and the languages involved. You can get the computer to count the translated words. This word count is usually provided at the end of a spell check. Unfortunately, there is little or no comparable ratio that can be applied to all word processing packages. The only advice I can offer is agree with the client in advance on how you are going to charge.

Some translators are in favour of charging according to target language words. There is a good argument for this since you can get the computer program to do a word count for you. The difficulty is quoting to a client on the basis of source language words. It is possible to apply a conversion factor but the resultant target language total depends on how verbose, or otherwise, the translator is.

Other methods are applied to charging. These include per line or per page. The difficulty is however deciding 'What is a standard line?' or 'What is a standard page?' Some jobs need to be estimated because the sheer volume of words would make word counting tiresome if it is just for a quotation. If the pages in a text are reasonably homogenous, it is possible to provide a reasonably accurate estimation by working out the average word count per page using, say, five representative pages and then multiplying this by the total number of pages.

You will gradually get a feel for the conversion rate in the language pair(s) with which you work. You can then use the computer word count to check your estimate when your translation is complete.

4.5   Quotations

Giving a quotation for a job, sight unseen, is folly. Ask the client to fax a number of typical sample pages so that you can give a more accurate quotation subject to sight of the complete document. The average number of words per A4 page is around 300 but can vary from a few words up to 1000 if the page is typeset! The legibility of the text will also influence the speed at which you are able to translate. An extreme example of a text that was sent to me for translation is shown opposite. It had probably been faxed a couple of times before I had received it with deterioration of legibility as a result.

It is useful to set up some form of table for costing your work. I know this sounds bureaucratic but it gives you a structured approach and is a useful *aide memoire* for all the items for which you should charge. The rates and figures in the table below are merely examples for guidance. Ensure that the client is aware that VAT will be added where applicable. State also that the quotation is valid until a given date (say one month or three months ahead).

Miscellaneous charges include any costs incurred for items over and above what is normally included in the translator's normal fee. It is better to increase your rates slightly as a contingency measure rather than add on additional miscellaneous charges.

Try to avoid committing yourself to a fixed price or deadline for a translation without sight of the complete material. There will unfortunately be times when you miscalculate – this is inevitable. The example shown on the following page is what I received when I agreed to translate a single page of A4 text from a client. I had assumed about 300 words of legible text and had agreed delivery on the same day.

4.6   Working from home

This is a practical and obvious choice when you are starting up. Consider the legal implications carefully. Your rent, leasehold or freehold agreement may contain a clause or covenant which states that your home may not be used for commercial purposes. Your solicitor and accountant will be able to advise.

Try to use a room that is not required for any other purpose. You must be able to get away from the office at the end of the day. If a room is used solely for running your business, you are able to apportion the costs of heating and lighting the room as business expenses. you may be tempted to charge the business 'rent' for using part of your home. Again, ask the advice of your accountant. If you are not careful, you could end up paying

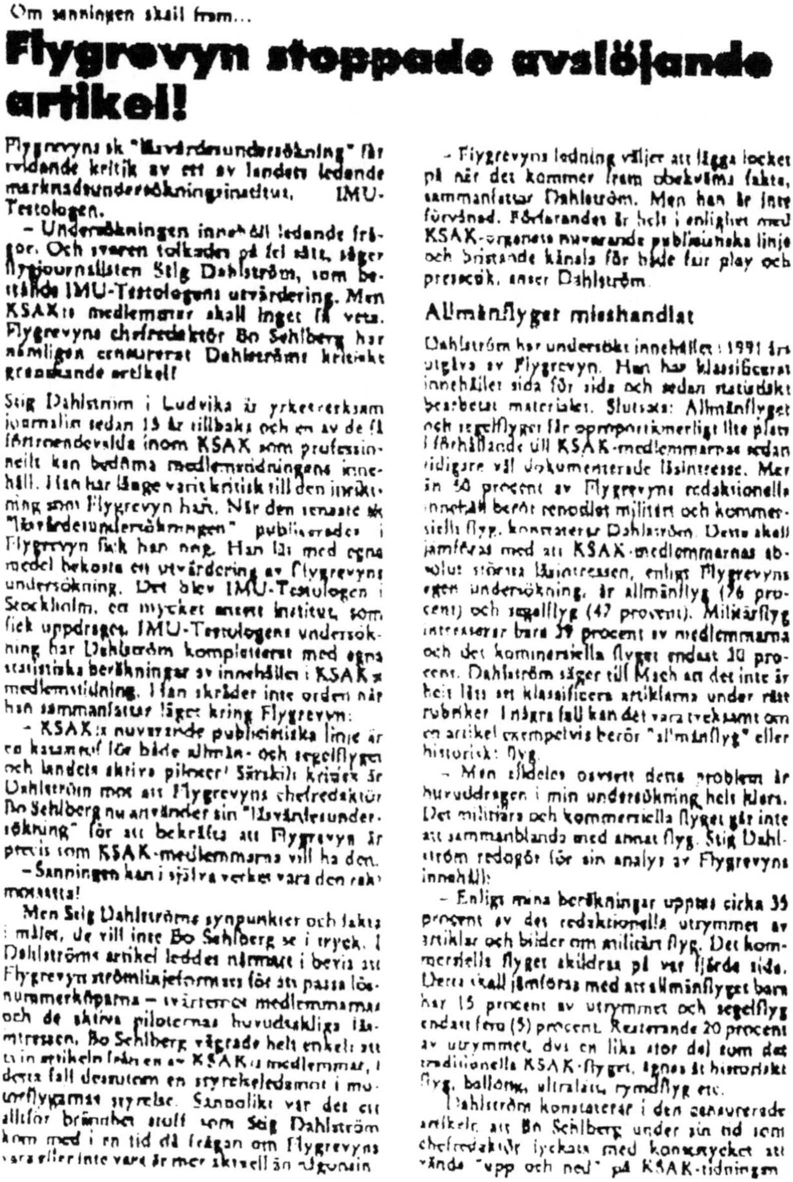

Figure 6. Example of almost illegible text submitted for translation

capital gains tax for that proportion of the house used as an office when you come to sell the property. You could also incur business rates for the room(s) used as an office.

4.7 Private or business telephone line?

If you have a single telephone line, trying to apportion private and business calls is an additional chore even though telephone bills in most areas are now itemised. Get a separate telephone line for your business if you can. This will obviate any disputes that might arise if you try to apportion your private telephone bill according to private and business calls. It will also allow you to ignore the business phone after hours and at weekends. You can of course get an answering machine but if you establish the fact that your business phone is answered only during working hours you will be able to enjoy your leisure time. It is very tempting to work all hours if the work is available but the quality of your work will suffer.

If the telephone line is registered as a business line, the initial cost and rental charges will be slightly higher than those paid by a private subscriber. The advantages are that response for any repairs will be quicker and you will automatically get a free entry in the Yellow Pages. Admittedly this will be a just single line but you will at least be listed in a directory that generates more enquiries than any other advertising medium.

4.8 Holidays

Holidays are not merely intended as a pleasure, they are an absolute necessity. If you get too engrossed in your work you can become dangerously tired without realising it. You need to recharge your batteries, get away from work and relax. If you spend too much time in your office you will get very tired of the place. If you work from home you'll feel that you can never get away from the office. Advise your clients in advance when you are going on holiday. They will respect the fact that you need to take a break and, if you have established a good working relationship, they will contact you again after your holiday.

4.9 Safety nets

Income protection
When working as a self-employed person, you must decide on the level of various insurances you wish to take out. What will happen if you become incapacitated and are unable to work? The benefit that you may derive from the state may not be sufficient to cover your outgoings. It is therefore worthwhile considering an income protection scheme to provide financial security if you are sick.

Private health insurance

The advantages of having this type of insurance is, again, a matter of personal choice. The benefits are self-evident. Being able to decide when you want to accept treatment facilitates business planning.

4.10 Dealing with salesmen

Salesmen have a job to do and that is selling consumables, services and commodities to people who have a perceived need. If a salesman is attempting to sell you something you do not want, be firm but polite and say '*No*' as soon as you can. You do not have to justify any reason for saying '*No*' – just stand your ground even though the sales pitch may be so convincing. Probably the most insistent people are sellers of stationery and advertising space.

You need stationery and, if you shop around, you can get reasonable discounts. Most major suppliers provide comprehensive catalogues which all seem to be about the same. Good discounts are usually offered on frequently-used items such as paper, fax rolls, computer disks and envelopes. Deliveries are usually prompt when you make an order (next day delivery if you fax an order before 4 in the afternoon). Check whether the supplier makes a delivery charge for an order below a certain amount. Bulk buying is of course cheaper and it may be worth clubbing together with a colleague to get a good deal.

4.11 Advertising

4.11.1 Yellow Pages and other published directories

You will need to advertise the fact that your services are available. The fact that you may be an excellent translator is of no avail if your potential clients have no idea of your existence.

You will automatically be listed in the Yellow Pages if you have a business telephone line. It is well worth having a slightly more imposing entry as soon as you can afford it.

If you become a member of the various professional associations for translators, you will be listed in the directories that these associations publish.

People who sell advertising space have a range of approaches which sound incredibly plausible to the unwary. Beware of the 'you have been specially chosen' or 'We are writing this editorial and are inviting a limited number of translation companies . . . .' approach. Be assertive. You do not have to listen to all the tempting arguments unless you want to. Interject firmly, and as soon as possible, but politely with 'I have a fixed budget for advertising that is already committed and the answer is No.' The counter argument is that you will not be billed until next year so you can include it in next year's budget. You can guarantee that the bill will arrive when you least expect it! (Practice saying '*No!*' out loud in as many ways as you can when you are on your own – it's quite easy.)

'One-off' adverts with the promise of editorial space seldom produce any response. The company I work for has made a careful analysis of response to the various forms of advertising we have purchased. The preferred form of paid advertising is in Yellow Pages. Your listing in the ITI or IoL directories is very useful if people are aware of these professional associations. Put yourself in your intended client's position and consider what you would do. In all probability you would pick up the Yellow Pages, go to the relevant classification, start at the beginning and look for the nearest entry in your locality that satisfies your criteria.

Beware of bogus 'proforma invoices' which present you with prepared adverts in some fax directory or otherwise that just require your approval and signature. They often look very convincing but are usually a confidence trick. If you do receive such invoices (usually mailed from mainland Europe) send them to your local Trading Standards Office or professional association.

4.11.2 E-commerce

The use of email and website has significantly changed and will continue to change the way the profession works. A translator's budget for traditional postal services, often referred to as 'snail mail' is declining in favour of email. The translator can now send his most of his translations by email – exceptions are where a translation needs to be certified and original documents sent or returned to the client.

The translator can publicise his services by subscribing to a number of electronic databases such as www.aquarius.net or by building a personal website and ensure that it has the appropriate keywords etc so that is can be searched for using search engines.

4.11.3 Sponsored advertising

There are times when you will be approached to provide sponsored advertising – usually for some worthwhile charity. I leave it to your own conscience whether or not to accept such requests. The usual format is to buy advertising space in a theatre programme for an event to raise funds for a particular charity. If you can accept that there will probably be no response to such advertising then you may still wish to go ahead. A word of caution, once you have accepted to advertise in one instance you may subsequently be approached by several more.

4.12   Financial considerations

Consult either your bank or an accountant before setting up. If you have prepared the ground with a budget, cashflow forecast and business plan, you will be taken far more seriously than if you were to walk into the bank unprepared with the bold statement, 'I want to start up a business as a translator – how much money will you lend me?'. Consider also whether you need to register for VAT. There is a turnover threshold above which you are obliged to register. It may be an advantage to register even if your turnover doesn't reach this level. The principal advantage of registering for VAT is that you can recover tax on all your purchases. Since your clients will probably be registered for VAT, it will make no difference to them if VAT is add to invoices. The disadvantage of being VAT registered is the additional paperwork and VAT returns that you are obliged to complete. There is also the thought that a VAT-registered business is generally viewed as being more 'substantial'.

Your budget and cashflow forecast may look fine on paper. You've worked out what you reckon to receive in fees and what you expect to pay out during the year. But, and this is a big **BUT**, income on paper is not the same as money in the bank! The amount of income tax you will need to pay will depend on individual circumstances. You may also wish to set aside an amount each month for pension provisions. The way you organise this will depend on your status in your organisation and the type of pension fund you wish to contribute to. Ask an accountant for advice.

There was a time at the beginning of my freelance career when I thought that if I worked hard enough and bought only the things I really needed then I would earn a living. I discovered after a while that this unstructured approach does not guarantee success. Let's work out a budget on the assumption that you work 22 days a month for 10½ months of the year. (*Don't forget Bank Holidays!*). You must also allow for holidays to recharge your batteries. Although you have the capacity to start translating straight away, there is the little matter of getting clients to do work for. In the budget forecast for the first twelve months of operation, I have assumed a gradual build-up over the first three months and that you take only two weeks holiday and public holidays during your first year.

Working steadily you should be able to produce 2000 words on average per day when you start as a freelance translator. Your rate will improve but let us consider a realistic work load. What you receive in fees is not your net income of course since there are the costs of running your business to consider. It could be helpful if you set up a budget on a monthly basis to show what you expect to earn and what you expect to purchase – and when such transactions will take place. You can then use this as a basis for working out what your cashflow is likely to be.

This budget is fairly hypothetical and does not take account of the fact that you will probably work far more than 'normal' hours and even at weekends. You must adjust the budget to suit your own capacity for work, the actual expenses that you feel you will incur, and the provisions you will need to make for income tax and other charges.

I have assumed that you have taken a bank loan (or overdraft) initially to purchase a PC with built-in modem and printer. These are essentials. This will probably continue into your second and third years in business as you purchase items such as a fax, photocopier (possibly) and scanner. You will also need some form of funding or income so that you can survive during the first twelve months of business. I have included a provision for professional services since you will need initial advice and help when starting up. Even though you may do your own book keeping, it is advisable to have a professional to deal with tax returns and correspondence with your tax officer. The tax authorities do publish a lot of useful information.

Cashflow

The initial finance you have available is the most important issue when setting up. This is particularly so during the early months before you start earning a sufficient income from the business. In effect, you will need to have some money available to start up in business.

The most important item to watch is your cashflow. You may have invoiced a client for a translation but, until you actually get paid, the income that the invoice represents will be on paper only and not in the bank. Profit is the difference between your income from translations and the cost of producing those translations and, as such, is recognised when you submit your invoice. But profit is not the same as cash. Profitable, expanding businesses can go bankrupt simply because they run out of cash.

If you talk to the bank or any other source of finance, you will inevitably be asked for a cashflow forecast. This shows when you expect to receive payment for your invoices and pay the various costs of running your business. You will also need to make provision for paying income tax, national insurance and VAT. This is easy if you have a spreadsheet program such as Excel.

To work out your cashflow you can assume that you will get 60% of your invoices paid in the month following the month in which you submitted your invoice, while the remaining 40% will be paid in the subsequent month. Some items such as telephone bills may be paid quarterly in arrears. You can apply the same analogy to your purchases. Taxes must be paid when they are due. I suggest you make an allowance each month for this and put the cash in a high-interest account until you receive a tax assessment.

You may not need to register for VAT initially but if you do you will need to include VAT charged to clients or paid to suppliers, and consider net VAT paid to or claimed back from Customs and Excise on a quarterly basis. Regulations governing VAT are fairly complex, particularly when dealing with companies abroad, so it is best to seek the advice and guidance of the VAT authorities. They are usually very helpful and have a number of publications available to explain your position. If you use a software package such as Sage Accountant, you will find all the necessary data in the software documentation.

I have kept the budget and discussion on cashflow as simple as possible. The most important message is, 'WATCH YOUR CASHFLOW'.

4.12.1 Getting paid

Translation is your livelihood and you *must* charge for the work you do. I know this sounds simple and obvious. Rates for translation are governed by the market and are fairly straightforward. What you must not neglect to do is to consider 'overtime rates' and additional work you may have to do, such as layout enhancement, and charge accordingly.

A client may ring late in the day with an 'urgent translation' that has to be done by a very tight deadline. Do not be reticent in quoting a premium for working unsociable hours. In some cases, the 'urgency' will be reappraised and a more reasonable deadline will be offered when the client is faced with additional charges. I have seen many examples where a client has completed a quotation for a project and has then asked for it to be translated in an unreasonably short space of time. He will have completed his part of the work and is 'now waiting for the translator'. Since the client's quotation will need to be submitted by a given time, you have no alternative but to comply.

Make sure you charge for working unsociable hours if this is requested by the client. What you charge is up to you to negotiate but I would suggest 50% extra if you have to work in the evening and 100% over the weekend.

The UK Government has introduced legislation to give businesses a statutory right to claim interest if another business pays its bills late. This legislation is called the Late Payment Of Commercial Debts (Interest) Act 1998. Small businesses have a statutory right to claim interest on debts incurred under contracts. This right is not compulsory.

The Act does not replace existing custom and practice. If the parties have undertaken business on the basis of usual industry practice , (for example, payment at the end of the month following the date of invoice), then this practice will probably still apply. However, if any remedy for late payment is 'not substantial' the terms of the Act will apply.

Where there is an agreed credit period the payment is late if it is made after the last day of the credit period. If no credit period has been agreed, then the Act sets a default period of 30 days after which interest can run. A user's guide can be downloaded by visiting the Better Payment Practice Group's website www.payontime.co.uk.

The EC Directive on combating late payment on commercial transactions (Directive 2000/35/EC) was formally adopted on 15 June 2000 and has to be implemented by all Member States by 8 August 2002.

4.12.2 Accounts

Your time is best spent doing what you are good at – translation. It is therefore an advantage to have an accountant to produce your year-end accounts and to deal with your tax matters. You can of course do your own book keeping and all the accountant will need to do at the end of the year is to go through the figures and decide what taxable deductions you ought to claim for and so on. He is much more experienced at dealing with the tax and other authorities. He is also able to advise you on the legal aspects of setting up a business.

4.12.3 Taxation

When you work as an employee, your employer deals with your taxation and national insurance contributions. When you are self-employed you need to make provisions for these costs yourself since you will be taxed in arrears. Set aside a fixed amount per month in an interest-bearing account and do not touch it however great the temptation may be. Be realistic and disciplined about how much you need to set aside. *The tax authorities have awesome powers.* You can ring your local tax office who are usually quite helpful.

4.12.4 Pensions

Retirement seems a long way off when you are starting your working life. As a professional you will enjoy a comfortable income level that will make a state pension look fairly small by comparison. Even a small monthly amount set aside will accumulate to provide a significant pension. It is also worth considering the tax allowance you get on pension payments. Again, your accountant or a pension broker can advise. A pension scheme is a form of savings and could provide security for a loan if needed at a later date. There are however severe restrictions that apply to the use of personal pension schemes as security.

4.13 Marketing and developing your services

Translations cannot be sold as a commodity even though some clients often feel that translations can be picked off the shelf as quickly as a packet of soap powder! You must identify a market need and then satisfy that need so that both you and the client derive some form of benefit.

The easiest way to get started is either get a job as a staff translator or to get work from agencies. There is considerable competition for translation work even though reports indicate that the amount of work world-wide is expanding at about 15% a year. It is therefore disheartening at times applying for work either as a staff translator or a freelance and having your approach either turned down or ignored. When you submit an application, present it in the best way you can – well-presented applications get remembered.

You will be competing against many other applicants and all translation agencies receive applications for work every day. I know from personal experience that the level of presentation ranges from well-produced CVs with a neat hand-written letter to photo-copied and barely-legible applications with address changes etc written by hand. Your presentation needs to have an immediate and convincing impact. If you do not check your application for accuracy, spelling mistakes or poor grammar, you are hardly likely to convince a work provider that you can produce accurate and correct target language texts.

Don't be disheartened by rejections. Try and remember that you are marketing a service and, if it is not to the client's liking, it is the service and not you personally that is being rejected.

Just consider the statistics applied by companies when they send out advertising material. If the mailing list is not targeted, the possible 'conversion rate' will probably be no more than 0.1%. Even if the marketing is reasonably targeted, the 'conversion rate' is not likely to be above a couple of percent.

Look at the job being advertised, or consider the possible needs of the agency, and carry out a personal SWOT analysis. List your **S**trengths, identify your **W**eaknesses (and try and strengthen them), look for **O**pportunities, and identify any **T**hreats. After all, marketing is matching your abilities to what the client needs so that you both achieve satisfaction and derive some financial benefit.

You need to establish yourself as a freelance and advertise the fact that you are available. Probably the best long-term advertising, or passive marketing, is to use the Yellow Pages. It will take some time for any passive advertising to take effect but, in the meantime, you can contact potential suppliers of translation work. The following are possible mailing targets:

- Translation companies and agencies
- Foreign embassies and consulates – the commercial attaché is a good contact
- International chambers of commerce
- Local chambers of commerce

How you actually prepare your publicity material is up to you. Unless you produce some form of printed promotional material, I would suggest a brief introductory letter with appendixes containing a CV, references and the language/subject combinations in which you feel confident. Note any major translation projects you may have worked on.

Most translation agencies have their own forms for you to fill in so be brief in your introductory letter to this target. What the agency will be initially interested in is whether you have sufficient qualifications and experience, what language combinations you offer, what subjects you feel confident with, the rates you charge, and what equipment you have.

4.13.1 An outline marketing strategy

You first need to identify the types of client you want to approach, and the geographical areas in which you will find them. Pick the easy targets, or 'cherry pick', rather than making a blanket approach. Decide on the strategy that you wish to adopt – cost leadership or differentiation. If you do not have special skills and experience that allow you to differentiate then you will need to offer the most competitive price. The latter is less rewarding but less effort. Ansoff's classic model illustrates this (Ref.6).

COMPETITIVE ADVANTAGE

	Lower cost	Differentiation
Broad	COST LEADERSHIP	BROAD DIFFERENTIATION
Narrow	COST FOCUS	DIFFERENTIATION FOCUS

Figure 7. Competitive scope versus competitive advantage

If you concentrate on differentiation then your competitive scope will be narrow but you will be able to charge a higher rate for your work. If you offer cost leadership, i.e. low prices, your competitive scope will be broader.

If you are dealing with companies abroad, you will be faced with the added dimension of exchange rates. You will also need to make a decision about which currency to use when you quote for work. There is no easy answer to this since circumstances change. If you have always quoted rates in GBP (£ sterling) you could always be sure that your rates were competitive and would stay that way since the £ has a history of weakening against other currencies. This situation changed significantly in 1997 as the £ strengthened against other currencies. A significant market for the company which I work for is Scandinavia and Sweden in particular. In the last couple of years the rate of exchange has moved from GBP1 = SEK 10.20 to GBP1 = SEK 15.80 at worst! This represents a significant price disadvantage.

This disadvantage can been combated in a number of ways:

1. reducing prices slightly but also profit margin – less than desirable
2. maintaining your differentiation focus and providing high quality work that needs little or no further processing

3. focusing on markets that do not present a cost disadvantage.

Clients will buy translations from you only if they are of intrinsic value or can add value to the products or services that the clients markets or sells. You have to convince the client that what you have to offer can provide this value. Consider the translation process and how this can provide or add value (Ref. 7).

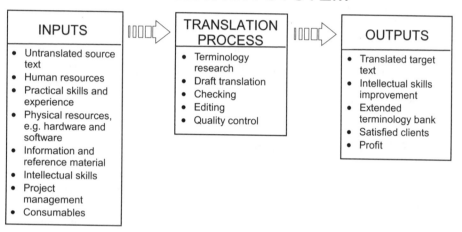

Figure 8. The translation process

4.13.2 Try not to put all your eggs into one basket

While a major contract may be very attractive, it is dangerous to over-extend yourself by putting all your resources into satisfying a single client. Endeavour to plan ahead and cultivate a number of clients that leave you with choices. Consider what could happen if you have worked for a single client for several weeks or more and then experience difficulty in getting paid. You will have turned down other assignments in the meantime and you become financially vulnerable. A reasonable adage is not to allow any single client to represent more than 25% of your turnover. It is worth remembering that once you have submitted an invoice, it will be considered an asset in your balance sheet and you will be taxed on it even though the invoice is not yet paid. Ideally you should be cultivating new clients so that you can try, at least, to maintain a steady workload. Experience will show which assignments and clients are most profitable.

4.13.3 Lifelong learning

Although there is ready access to a wealth of information on the Internet the application of that information benefits enormously from knowledge and experience that can be gained only from lifelong learning. In a profession that requires specialists as well as generalists you can enhance your competitive advantage and the quality and authority of your work by what can be generally termed continuous personal development.

For the fledgling translator fresh from university this may seem a daunting prospect. If you have gained an MA in translation studies you will have received a degree of exposure to subject modules that you have elected to study. But having spent say 50 hours in lectures on each subject module over the academic year plus additional hours on tutor-marked assignments is merely an introduction but could indicate to you what subjects really interest you. After all, translation should be challenging and rewarding. Making good translations is easier and enjoyable if the subject interests you and you feel confident with the quality of the result.

4.14   OK, where do you go from here?

The simple answer is to decide what you want to be at some time in the future, five years for example, and seriously consider how you are going to make the transition from your present level of skills.

The fast-track method is to go back to school. I know, this costs time and money and the last thing you want after having spent upwards of four years in full-time tertiary education is more school. But if you want to make a serious career as a translator you will need to offer some specialisation. If you manage to get a job as a staff translator (not in a translation company but in industry) you may automatically gain specialist knowledge through day-to-day contact with more experienced colleagues.

Any company worth its salt will want its staff to be well-trained and will be prepared to consider skills development. There are the cynics who say, 'Why should my company pay for further training if all the person will do is to look for better paid jobs elsewhere. There are several arguments to counter this attitude.

- Is it not better to have a well-trained person more a year than an untrained person for a long time?
- Salaries, while important, are seldom the prime reason why people look for jobs elsewhere.
- Most members of staff are usually loyal to their employer – a virtue that needs to be reciprocated – and do not join a company with the intention of leaving within a short space of time.

There are many opportunities for continued personal development. Your local college will certainly offer a broad range of courses to suit your own personal interests. Though I hate book-keeping I now have a reasonable understanding of the subject after having attended evening classes at my local college. From my own experience I feel that distance learning is the most practical for long-term courses. It requires discipline and dedication, and the support of your partner and family. It also allows you a degree of flexibility since you can do your studies at times to suit your translation commitments and lifestyle. I successfully completed an MBA this way.

One of the dangers of working as a freelance translator is lack of physical contact with the outside world. It is all too easy to conduct all your business by telephone, fax and email without ever seeing your customers be they agencies of direct clients. Use all the networking opportunities you can to meet people outside the profession.

5 The translator at work and the tools of the trade

'A desk is a wastepaper basket with legs.'
Anon.

5.1 Your working environment

Normal physical work requires alternate tensioning and relaxation of muscles for blood circulation to function satisfactorily. When a muscle is subjected to static loading, i.e. long term loading without relaxation, the muscle is tense and circulation is hampered thus causing tiredness. The greater the load, the quicker tiredness occurs.

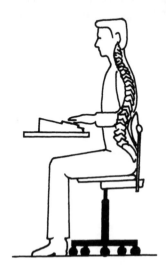

Neck straight
Shoulders relaxed
Upper arms vertical
Right angle between upper arms and
forearms
Slight 'S' shape to backbone
Sit squarely on the seat
Lower legs vertical
Feet flat on the floor

Figure 9. Correct working posture

To prevent muscular tiredness, your working environment should be arranged in such a manner that you can work comfortably at the different aspects of translation work. Legroom should be sufficient so that leg movement is not restricted by table or desk legs, cupboards or drawers. It is also very important to choose a chair that provides adequate adjustment.

Muscle problems are caused not only by the sedentary work of translation but, more often than not, by sitting incorrectly. You should endeavour to maintain the natural curvature of your spine with a curve at the neck and the lumbar region. In this way, the vertebrae in your back will be subjected to an even pressure and the muscles around your spine will not become strained. The following are general points of advice on how to sit:

- Try to keep your neck straight since this facilitates the supply of blood to your neck muscles.
- Do not work with your shoulders raised – try to keep them relaxed.
- Keep your upper arms vertical.
- Keep your forearms at right angles to your upper arms.
- Your hands should be straight in relation to your forearms.
- Try to maintain the natural S curve of your spine.
- Sit squarely on the seat of the chair.
- Keep your lower legs vertical.
- Keep your feet flat on the floor.

If you do have problems, it is worthwhile talking to a physiotherapist. He can advise you if the ergonomics of your working environment are incorrect and if there are any exercises that can be beneficial. The way in which you furnish and arrange your working environment has a considerable impact on your efficiency at work and your health. The effects of repetitive strain injury (commonly known as RSI) take a long time to make themselves felt. They may be so bad as to actually prevent you from working.

Do not sit in front of your computer for hours at a time. Discipline yourself to work for no more than one hour at a time and then take a break. Get away from your desk and stretch your muscles. Even though you may be working on an extremely urgent job, your mind and body need to relax now and again to perform efficiently.

My practice is to set a timer for 50 minutes and then take at least a five minute break. Your level of continuous efficiency will be maintained and your body will be less affected by sitting in a stationary position for hours at a time. It is worth noting that the lumbar region of your back experiences three times as much loading in a sitting position compared with when you stand. At worst you may experience disk problems that may prevent you from working and may eventually require surgery.

You may feel that you need to do exercises. Consider the fact that you will be sitting in the same position for a considerable period making repeated movements with your hands and fingers. If you do not do elementary exercises but remain sedentary you run a considerable risk of RSI. This may be felt in different ways as a pain in the back of the neck or as a burning sensation at the back of your rib cage, depending on how you have developed the injury. There is also the argument that if you are physically fit then your mental stamina is enhanced. There is nothing worse than being mentally tired, and it takes a lot longer to recover from this type of fatigue than it does to recover from physical tiredness.

5.2   Arranging your equipment

It is worth getting a proper desk with sufficient desktop area for your PC, reference books and other accoutrements. Get the best chair you can possibly afford otherwise your work will literally become a pain in the neck or back. There are shops that sell secondhand office furniture, some of which may be genuine bankrupt stock. This will allow you to purchase your basic furniture at a fraction of the cost of new items. The ergonomics of your workplace are something you must decide upon yourself. There are certain fundamentals that will make matters easier:

• Make sure your computer is in a comfortable position and correctly adjusted so that there is no glare from the screen or reflections on the screen that make reading difficult.
• Adjust your chair to the most ergonomic height and make sure you have proper lighting.
• A document holder will facilitate reading the text to be translated. Alternate the position of your document holder from left to right at regular intervals. This will prevent you from turning your head in the same direction when you switch between document and screen.

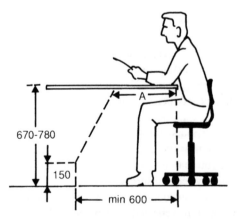

A = At least 450 mm for a printer table or worktop, and at least 300 mm for a terminal desk

Figure 10.   Correct angle of vision

• Your screen should be arranged so that your line of sight is at right angles to the screen and at an angle of 20° below the horizontal. The distance between your eyes and the screen should allow you to read the characters with ease. A suitable distance is 70 cm.

5.3   Eye problems

Eye problems can occur when looking at the same object for long periods. In the case of prolonged and intensive work on screen, it is a good idea to have some other object in the vicinity, such as a picture or poster, so that you can direct your eyes elsewhere occasionally so they can relax.

Simple eye exercises

Allow your eyes to relax now and again. Relax them by changing focus and directing your gaze towards a distant object. Change what you are doing if you can so that you do not spend long periods in front of the screen. Close your eyes tightly while taking one or two deep breaths.

If you wear glasses, consult your optician to see whether you need special lenses when working at your terminal.

It helps your eyes if the screen has dark characters against a light background. An anti-glare filter can also help. Make sure that the screen is properly focused otherwise you could get a severe headache after an hour or so. In extreme cases you may also develop the sensation of having sand in your eyes. You can replace or adjust your screen but you have but one pair of eyes.

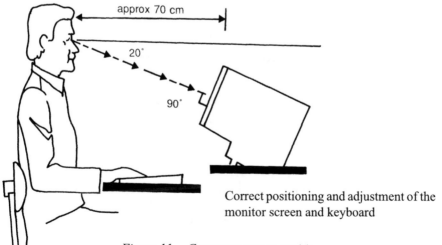

Correct positioning and adjustment of the monitor screen and keyboard

Figure 11.   Computer screen position

5.4   Buying equipment

Buying equipment is a hazardous exercise. Talk to a fellow translator or two and try to get unbiased advice before parting with your cash. You can benefit by listening to the experiences of others – preferably somebody who has been using computers for a while. Technology changes uncomfortably fast some times. Before considering what tools are available today, it might be interesting to compare the tools of, say, 20-odd years ago. A

Element	1974	2003
Professional status	Mostly academics using linguistic skills. Very few people with formal skills or training in translation theory and practice.	Evolving recognition that proper translation requires practitioners who are trained and skilled in the art. Minimum requirements are a degree in modern languages and computer literacy. Universities and colleges offer postgraduate courses in translation theory and practice.
Tools of the trade	The correctable golfball typewriter was the advanced technology of the time. Translations were delivered by mail or by hand. Only large companies had what are termed dedicated systems that could offer basic text processing facilities.	Few translators are able to work without a computer, modem and fax that offer facilities such as: • computer-aided translation (translation memory systems) and terminology management • advanced formatting • extensive editing features • spell checking • glossary compilation • business management • electronic mail
Typesetting	Work passed to typesetter whose skills were expensive and who needed to retype the text completely.	Typesetting can be performed by the translator – this is known as desktop publishing, or DTP. As an alternative, the work to be typeset can be transmitted electronically to the photosetter who reformats the text without having to retype.
Communication	Postal service, couriers, telex, personal delivery, or primitive fax machines	Postal service, couriers, fax and, above all, electronic mail.
Skills	Linguistic ability and editorial skills. Ability to type.	Linguistic ability and editorial skills, keyboarding skills, computer literacy. Ability to deliver and receive work electronically. Specialised subject knowledge.

Table 7.   Tools of the trade, 20+ years ago and now

very thick book could be written on this subject since, like many other professions, the advent of computers has had a profound influence on the way people work.

Incidentally, the word 'compatible' is dreadfully misused. You will need to communicate electronically with clients and the amount of time that is wasted and the level of frustration generated through the use of so-called 'compatible' equipment is unbelievable. But don't let this put you off. Most things are easy when you know how.

Consider the equipment you will need:

- Computer
- Printer
- Software to produce your work and to manage your business
- Photocopier
- Fax
- Modem (usually integral in new PCs).

Since these are of central importance to the way the translator works, they are dealt with separately in the next chapter.

There are other items of equipment that are essential and others that can make your working life more tolerable.

5.4.1 Computer

Translation companies use PCs and Macintosh machines since the company's clients used both systems. However, my experience as a former head of a translation company indicates that approximately 90% of translations were produced on PCs and the rest on Macintosh machines. The latter ran programs favoured by publishers and printers. This would indicate that the safer bet is to invest in a PC.

Prices vary enormously depending on the configuration you want. I would recommend that you buy the best you can buy with the highest specification screen you can afford. After all, you will be spending a fair proportion of your work day looking at the screen As a minimum I would suggest the following computer specification:

- 20 GB hard disk (the information storage capacity of the machine)
- 256 MB RAM (Random Access Memory).
- CD-ROM drives with the facility to write to CDs.
- A processor with a fast clock speed of 1 GHz (the speed at which the computer works) – at the time of writing the fastest models run at about 2 GHz
- Built-in high speed modem
- The appropriate ports to connect a mouse, keyboard, software dongle, etc.

(The recommendation in the first edition of this book, first published in April 1993 was for 40 MB hard disk, 4 MB RAM, 386 processor and a clock speed of 16 MHz!)

At lot of software packages occupy a large chunk of your hard drive. Consider that you may wish to add other programs such as accounts, database, and spreadsheet packages, all of which may occupy very large chunks of your hard disk. So, being realistic, 20 GB is probably the minimum you will need. Many Windows-based programs require around 20 MB of free RAM to operate – the fact that a machine has 256 MB of RAM does not mean that this capacity is at your disposal! The more programs you have open the slower your machine will operate. Consider also how you are going to store all your translation files.

Shop around and look in the computer magazines to get the best deal. And don't be shy in asking for discounts. You should be able to get a reasonable machine with the above specification for around £1200 + VAT depending on the configuration and the type of monitor you choose. Note that some prices are quoted without monitors. The price will include an operating system such as Windows XP which, although you cannot operate without it, will not do anything but provide a range of basic utilities. You could call it the brain of the machine which, with specific software, will get the computer to perform the tasks you want it to do. Many machines are now sold with 'bundled software'. In other words you get a choice of programs that will already be installed when your machine is delivered.

The least expensive way to purchase a new computer is to buy at the 'cash-and-carry' establishments that are now gaining ground. Once you have purchased your machine, there will be nobody to hold your hand and to guide you through the initial operations required to set your system up. Dealers who do the installation and setup for you obviously make a charge for the work they do and this is reflected in the higher price level. 'Cash-and-carry' is an option worth considering once you have had some experience of operating a computer.

The quality of documentation supplied with programs has improved over the years but often leave a lot to be desired. Most programs are fairly intuitive and have help screens to guide you.

There are of course portable computers that are also very attractive. They are much more expensive than 'desk-top' computers and are not, in all honesty, a realistic option for a beginner. This assumes that you do not need to travel around and provide your own equipment.

5.4.2   Printer

The printer you buy will depend on the level of presentation either you or your clients demand. In many cases you may send a translation to your client by modem thereby obviating the need to deliver a physical document.

It is however difficult, if not impossible, to manage without a printer. Even though you can see your text presented on screen, it is very difficult to proof-read without having a printout. Naturally the facilities the printer provides will be limited and the more features you demand the more your printer will cost.

The cost of laser printers has fallen dramatically since they were first introduced. The first such printer I purchased cost almost £4000 in 1990. It offered a range of fonts and reproduced print and graphics at about five pages a minutes with a resolution of 300 dpi (dots per inch). The inkjet colour printer I now use prints around twelve pages a minute with a resolution of 600 dpi. It cost less than £300 when purchased three years ago and has printed in the region of 45,000 pages since then.

5.4.3 Software to produce your work and to manage your business

Most people naturally become familiar with the system they have used for some time be it a PC or a Macintosh. I have worked on a number of systems on mainframe computers, networks, stand-alone PCs and Macintosh. Each word processing program I have worked with has its advantages and disadvantages. Thus any recommendation on which word processing software to use is fraught with danger. However, looking at the statistics of the work I have done over the last five years, I can see that the majority of my translations have been produced using Word for Windows.

The software I use as a freelance translator is as follows:

Software	Application
Microsoft XP	Computer operating system
Microsoft Word	Text processing
Microsoft Excel	Text processing of translation assignments such as annual reports Maintaining my own production record and monitoring cashflow
Microft Powerpoint, Microsoft Visio, Lotus Freelance	Graphics packages for editing client graphics embedded in translations
TRADOS Translator's Workbench and MultiTerm	Translation memory and terminology management systems for computer-aided translation
Internet Explorer	Online terminology research
Electronic dictionaries and reference sources on CD	Online terminology research
PageMaker	Translating manuals written in this format

5.4.4 Miscellaneous items

Answering machine

If you are working in isolation, there will be times when you are either not able or do not wish to answer the phone. There are few people nowadays who are reluctant to respond to an answering machine and if you leave a clear message that you will reply as soon as you return you will save people redialling unnecessarily. Put yourself in the position of a potential client and consider what is preferable – no reply, or at least the chance to receive/leave an informative message?

Basic stock of stationery and office consumables

It is of course not necessary to buy a whole stock of consumables at once. Try to open an account with one of the commercial stationery suppliers rather than buying from a local shop. A local shop may charge up to three times what you would need to pay as a result of buying directly from one of the many wholesale suppliers.

It is surprising how much paper you consume so 'bulk buying' can save money. Most major suppliers have a list of standard consumables such as paper, disks, and laser cartridges at very favourable prices. Having an account also means that you do not have to fork out for the goods directly. Nor do you have to make the physical effort of going to the shop to get your supplies. Some translators have formed loose cooperatives when buying supplies to gain the financial advantages offered by bulk buying.

Photocopier

This may perhaps not be at the top of your shopping list. The time will no doubt come when you feel it would be more practical to have your own copier than having to go to your local print shop. You will have to decide when the cost of getting your own copier outweighs the inconvenience of relying on an outside service. Having your own copier will cost you around £600 to buy. Good ex-demonstration machines or those traded in for upgrades are often good deals. But make sure you know what you're getting and what after-sales support is provided.

Salesmen often make very tempting offers based on a 'per-copy' cost. The idea is that you work out an assumed monthly consumption and then sign a deal on this basis. In all probability you will be charged for this amount irrespective of what you actually use so your actual 'per-copy' cost may be a lot more than you had originally anticipated. *Caveat emptor!* Fortunately there have been a number of articles criticising this practice and it does seem to be on the decline.

Fax

The quickest way a client can get a hard copy of a text for translation to you is probably by fax and the quality of reproduction is usually sufficient for the purpose. You can also return your translation in the same way if the quality of reproduction is acceptable. (The original can be sent by mail if necessary.) This practice has been largely superseded by electronic mail.

If your client is sending a large job that is urgent and is not available in electronic format, the first few pages can be sent by fax so that you can get started on the work. The complete job can then be sent by mail. If you have any specific queries, you can fax them to your client thereby giving him more time to resolve them.

If you intend working for agencies you will probably not even be considered for assignments if you do not have ready access to a fax machine and modem. Texts need to be sent to you quickly and confidentially so relying on a bureau will eventually become impractical.

A fax machine will cost upwards of £400 to buy and, at a push, will operate as a single-sheet photocopier. What you will need to pay will depend on the specification you demand.

Again, software is becoming increasingly versatile and Microsoft Office includes fax software that allows you to receive faxes on your computer for printing out. Such transmission is almost immediate.

Again, it might be interesting to reflect on how technology has developed. The first fax machine I purchased was a Group 2 machine that took about 2 minutes to receive a page. It used special paper that needed to be attached to a rotating drum, one sheet at a time. I needed to load the paper and then tell the sender to start transmitting. The drum started to rotate when communication was established and a stylus travelled across the rotating drum and heat-etched the surface of the paper. I can still recollect the burning smell that pervaded the office!

Modem

Most professional translators would find it difficult to work without modem facilities. A modem allows you to send a soft copy of your translation directly from your computer to the client's computer at any time (assuming his modem is set up to receive incoming files). It is frustrating having to rely on outside agencies such as the postal service and couriers so having a modem will allow you much more freedom of action.

I presently use a built-in ISDN mobile for electronic mail and internet services. Without these I am lost and it soon becomes apparent how dependent we have become on such services if, for some reason or another, they are temporarily unavailable.

Broadband facilities that used ADSL are becoming more available but availability is limited according to your location. Present technology does not permit the installation of broadband if you are more than 5 km from the relevant exchange. This 5 km is not the geographical distance but the length of the route taken by the cabling.

Scanners

As the name implies, a scanner is used to scan a piece of artwork, a photograph or text. It then converts what it sees to information that can be displayed on a screen or saved on disc. The operation of a scanner is briefly as follows: a light source is shone on the image to be scanned. The light that is reflected from the scanned document is detected by a light sensor (known as a charged coupled device or CCD) in the scanner. The varying signal this sensor gives is interpreted by the scanner controller. There are two types of scanner – hand-held and flatbed.

A hand-held scanner is moved manually across the area you wish to scan keeping it as steady as possible. This type of scanner is not normally suitable for optical character recognition since it is almost impossible to move a hand-held scanner steadily across an image without some distortion. The scanner is roughly T-shaped with the top bar housing the scanning head and the upright making up the handle. This type of scanner can normally scan half the width of an A4 page.

A flat bed scanner looks rather like the top half of a photocopier. The scanning head covers the whole width of the bed and scans the document in a steady controlled movement. A flatbed scanner is better for scanning full pages of text or graphics but, as in the case of some photocopiers, there may be some distortion towards the edge of the paper when scanning a book page near the spine.

A measure of the scanner's ability to produce graphics, in addition to its resolution, is the number of grey scales that can be recognised and reproduced. 256 is sufficient to reproduce most monochromatic images. In about 75% of the cases, scanners are sold together with the relevant software as a package and prices range from around £100 but you will also need text conversion software if you want to convert a graphical image to text that you can use in Microsoft Word for example.

The cost of a scanner and software must be set in proportion to the use and benefits you can derive. It has obvious applications if you work with desk top publishing. A further application is to scan pages of text to save having to retype them. This is worth considering if you are going to start your own translation company since there are many times when urgent translations are received from freelances by fax and require correction, amendment or reformatting. Having to retype text in an unfamiliar language is time-consuming and not at all easy. Scanning an unfamiliar language is perhaps not advisable since a lot of post-scanning editing may be required. Again, such editing should be done by a translator with the appropriate language skills.

Speech recognition software

Companies such as IBM and Philips have developed systems that can interact with the human voice. Claims state that the software can accept text being dictated at 70 to 100 words per minute. Each word no longer needs to be spoken as a discrete utterance to be recognised as was the case when the previous edition of this book was written. If words are properly recognised then there is no need to carry out a spell check. The manufacturers claim that their systems can choose correctly between like-sounding words such as 'to', 'two' and 'too', or 'our' and 'hour'.

The cost of speech recognition systems has decreased dramatically over the last few years. The level of sophistication has improved but the user still needs to spend a significant amount of time 'teaching' the software to recognise what is being said. You will get some strange results but, even if you are dictating proper names that are not translated, you can still get the software to recognise them providing you 'teach' the memory. I remember one example when I dictated the name of a Norwegian – Knut Frostad. The speech recognition system reproduced this as 'convicted full stop' – not a desirable result!

Phones

My office phone is fitted with a headset. This offers a number of advantages:

- I can work with your hands free while discussing edits or changes with your customer.
- You can continue working while somebody has put me 'on hold' for a while.
- I can resolve technical queries concerning your computer or software and have both hands free to take corrective action while still talking to whoever is providing the technical support.
- I can be marketing over the phone while at the same time filling in customer database information on screen.

I have a mobile phone but I use it entirely for my convenience. This includes calling my answering machine if I am away from my office (even when I am abroad) thereby maintaining contact.

Bits and pieces

Items such as a document holder are useful and you and you can decide yourself how comfortable and convenient you want to make your workplace.

There are other quite desirable pieces of equipment but, unless you can honestly justify their cost, they are not really worth considering. It's very tempting to buy sophisticated equipment but it is best to start with the bare essentials and gain some experience before committing your earnings for some way ahead. Buying 'add-on goodies' is also tempting but often a very unsatisfactory compromise. The well-rehearsed sales pitch of a dealer can sound very plausible but is no comfort once you have parted with your money and you are stuck with a piece of equipment that isn't quite what you wanted.

5.5   What does it all cost?

The 'essential' items represent quite a large investment (around £3,400 in 2002). You can use a local bureau for fax and photocopying services and the cost of these services must be weighed against the convenience of having your own equipment. However the less you need to rely on outside services the better. Note that you must also make allowance for an initial stock of items such as stationery, disks, postage stamps, and standard software such as Microsoft Office plus an email communications package.

Item	Cost (£)
Office furniture	300
Personal computer	1,200
Printer	300
Standard software	600
Fax (dedicated)	400
Copier	600
Answering machine	60
Total	3,460

Table 8.   Standard equipment in the translator's office

The range of equipment available on the market is enormous and it would be folly to try and list all the options in this book. Read the computer magazines and talk to colleagues.

You must also take into account what it will cost to have your equipment serviced and maintained. Annual maintenance usually works out at around 10% of the capital cost of the equipment. Check what warranty is provided with any equipment. You may get charged a lower price when you buy your equipment but you may find out that the warranty period is shorter and you need to start paying maintenance at an earlier date.

5.6   Purchasing your initial equipment

There are not too many budding translators who are able to afford to buy their initial equipment outright. If you have been working as a staff translator and plan to go freelance at some later date, you will perhaps be in the position to set aside funds over a period to finance your initial period in business on your own.

In all probability you will need assistance in financing your original purchases. What you will also need is a business plan with a cash flow forecast. This is not so much to convince your bank manager with hypothetical figures, but to assure yourself that you will be able to survive in business on your own. You will also need to consider what you can offer as security for a loan. Unsecured loans or overdrafts are much more expensive than secured loans. Ask the bank to explain all the options and go armed with a realistic business plan.

Leasing is an option that can also be considered. It is, however, seldom available immediately to people who are starting up in business as a sole trader. There are certain tax advantages offered by this form of financing. The options are usually lease-rental, where you do not own the equipment at the end of the period, and lease purchase where you do in fact purchase the equipment.

Leasing rates do of course differ according to the option you choose. Rates are usually quoted as £XX/month or quarter per £1000 lease capital that is arranged. Payment per quarter, rather than monthly, usually works out marginally cheaper. Present figures are around £34/£1000 per month for a 3-year lease. The rate depends on whether your agreement is for lease/rental or lease/purchase. Check what you are letting yourself in for before committing pen to paper.

Rates offered by leasing companies compare favourably with bank lending rates. There is also the argument that if you have used up your borrowing capacity at the bank then you have no further borrowing option. If you lease in preference to borrowing from the bank initially, you would be treated perhaps more favourably by the bank at a later date if you needed to raise capital quickly.

Talk to your accountant so that he can advise you what the real costs are and who owns the equipment at the end of the lease period.

5.7   Ways of working

5.7.1   Dictating translations

Dictation using a dictation machine as opposed to speech recognition software is a method of translation used by a small number of translators. It has advantages and disadvantages. An experienced translator is able to dictate around 2000 words an hour (about 30 minutes of actual playback time) but being able to dictate more than 6000 words a day, regularly, is extremely demanding. It does mean however than you can hand over the job of typing your translations to a skilled audio typist. If you can find a competent person with whom you can work, the option can be very productive.

I worked in this way for many years with an audio typist. Our combined output was in the region of 60,000 words a month, allowing time for checking and correcting. You do have the responsibility for an additional person and if he or she is off sick you need to have contingency resources at your disposal.

There are translators who dictate their translations and then type from their own dictation. This does permit you to make editorial changes while you are listening to the tape but, to me at least, seems a less than economical use of resources. There are odd occasions when a client specifically requests dictated work for security reasons but these are very much in the minority.

When I started working as a freelance translator, I wrote out my translations by hand. They were then given to a copy typist who gave me a draft to edit. I was reluctant to make major changes since I was aware of the additional work this meant for the typist. I was able to write about 300 words an hour. If you consider the time required for proof reading, I suppose the effective rate was around 200 words an hour. I then progressed to dictating tapes which were then transcribed by an audio typist. Our combined effective rate went up to around 1000 words an hour, including proof reading and editing. Working directly on a PC, I consider my effective translation rate to be in the region of 320 words an hour – a rate that I can sustain for most of a working day. It is of course possible to achieve much faster rates for short periods but experience has taught me to be realistic.

You will also need to consider the cost of dictation equipment for yourself and possibly for the person who is doing the audio typing for you. You must also consider compatibility of audio tapes if you use the services of a word processing bureau. Gründig dictation tapes have a capacity of 30 minutes on a single-sided tape, Philips dictation tapes have a capacity of 2 × 15 minutes on a two-sided tape. Other machines use standard cassette tapes with a capacity of 2 × 30 minutes and upwards.

5.7.2   Overtyping preformatted texts

This way of working is used in cases where translation memory tools cannot readily be used. This is particularly so for annual reports produced using a spreadsheet program such as Excel although more recent editions of translation memory software are able to handle this type of software. The usual reason is to comply with a specific layout that may be extremely complex and retain macros that perform financial calculations. Using a text already on disk will also save the drudgery of retyping and checking figures, lines of computer source text etc. that do not require translation but still need inclusion.

This type of translation is very time-consuming if you are not experienced. Your charges must also be amended according to the additional hours you spend on the work. There are ways of reducing the work that needs to be done if you make careful use of the 'search and replace' function in a word processing package. Use the facility with caution to make allowance for upper and lower case letters and other traps. Check whether your word processing package has the facility to create macros. If it does, you can use them to carry out global replacement operations. This can be applied to common words or phrases if used carefully.

Make sure that you have the hard copy in front of you in case you delete something before you have translated it. You will need to exercise your editing skills if the translated text must fit into a given space on a sheet of paper.

You may very occasionally need to use a graphics program that allows you to change text in a figure. The parallel use of Microsoft Word and Powerpoint or Visio is one example. Importing and exporting graphics files requires a degree of experience and should not be attempted until you feel really at home with your hardware and software.

A further application of this skill is when translating lines of computer 'source text'. You may, for example, have an instruction in English where the translation needs to be contained within a fixed number of characters. Problems arise when abbreviations cannot be translated. Software writers may not be aware that a program could eventually be translated and consequently do not make allowance for expansion of the number of characters required.

5.7.3 Using computer-aided translation (CAT)

This is also referred to as translation memory systems since all past translation saved in the computer's memories can be re-used if exact or near-matches (known as fuzzy matches) can be retrieved. I'll refer to them as CAT systems for brevity.

There are occasions when you might be asked to quote for translation work that is required in an unrealistically short space of time. The only feasible way of completing such work in a conventional way would be to use a team of translators working concurrently, and skilful project co-ordinators. The alternative is to develop CAT facilities where the computer produces a draft and then uses human post-translation editors to revise the work.

Development has been slow since the first serious attempts at machine translation were made 50 or more years ago (1948). These attempts were limited by contemporary hardware and other factors. The facility is becoming more of a viable option but still needs a skilled translator or language editor to make the result acceptable.

CAT software is essentially a set of tools used to manipulate a database of language information. It is the input of information in the form of translated words, phrases, sentences and even complete paragraphs in the source and target languages that constitutes this database. Potential benefits include:

- repetitive or similar texts need be translated only once,
- once glossaries have been entered in the system, future translations will always be consistent providing the translator selects the option offered by the terminology management system,
- greater speed of draft translation, thereby allowing more time for quality control,
- a computer can work on draft translation at any time of the day, thus a 10,000 word translation that would take a human translator about a week to produce could be done

overnight ready for editing the next morning. (Speeds of up to 10,000 words per hour have been claimed),
- reduction in production costs, thereby producing greater profitability,
- better quality control since text already entered in the software will not need to be re-checked if it can be identified uniquely.

CAT software is now available from a number of manufacturers of which the most-widely used is probably TRADOS. Such software is still reasonably expensive and requires a fairly powerful computer if it is to work satisfactorily. It is not something that you can use from day 1 since it needs a considerable amount of data input before it will start to produce anything like a usable translation. Try it when you first install it and you will get some hilarious results. However, the more information you can add the faster and better it works.

It is a misconception held by some unenlightened clients that all the translator needs to do is load the electronic file containing the source text into the computer and wait for the finished translation to be produced automatically. The following illustrates what happens in reality.

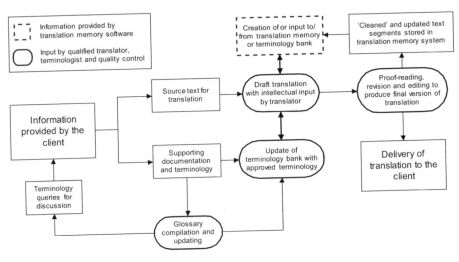

Figure 12. Input from CAT software in the translation process

6 Sources of reference, data retrieval and file management

'In all things, success depends on previous preparation,
and without such preparation there is sure to be failure.'
Confucius, c.550–c.478 BC

The sources of reference available on the Internet are incredible. For example, if you go to www.google.com, one of the popular search engines it will give you access to more than 2 billion pages! Just image what that would be in terms of books.

While you will be asked to translate a range of subjects, and you have all this information at your fingertips, you must accept that you have limitations. But having have authoritative references available your work will be made a lot easier.

Always ask if reference material is available when you accept a translation assignment. There may even be previous translations on the subject which provide a useful source of terms and vocabulary. You may need to adhere to an accepted 'house' style but, if you are not aware of this, you may produce a perfectly acceptable translation but it may be 'the wrong colour'.

There are times when there are no references available. There are also unhelpful clients who reply *'You're the translator – you should know!'* in response to a request for assistance. Fortunately, such clients are in the minority.

There is also a risk if you work as a freelance for a large company that the person commissioning the translation may not be aware of what is available within the company. This is particularly the case where the work is done under a time constraint. Ask if the company has a library and, if so, whether you may use it.

Try and get the name of a contact who is able to explain any problem, technical or otherwise, in the source language. If you can offer an explanation to another contact in the target language, you can usually get the correct term.

6.1 Dictionaries

You will probably be familiar with the standard bilingual dictionaries in your chosen language(s). It is possible to spend a lot of money on dictionaries that are of no real help.

Having said that, there are excellent dictionaries that provide terminology in specialist subjects. The best advice I can offer with regard to what dictionaries you should acquire is to talk to experienced translators or the Librarian of the Institute of Linguists (if you are a member).

Do not overlook the value of monolingual dictionaries in the source languages and their corresponding companion volumes in the target language. Although you may not immediately know the translation of a word and cannot find it in a bilingual dictionary, the explanation or definition in a monolingual dictionary is often very helpful particularly if it provides a simile that may be more familiar. Using Latin or Greek as a common denominator is well worth considering if you need to translate a medical or biological term.

One of the most demanding types of translation, I find, is that of translating restaurant menus. Many of the recipe names are products of the chef's imagination or may be regional names that almost defy translation if they are not to lose their impact completely. I recently translated a book on regional recipes in Sweden that included *nävegröt* and for which the instructions included 'Take a fistful of porridge'. I translated this recipe as *Fist porridge!* What I do when I am totally devoid of inspiration is to use the best equivalent in French. This is usually far more acceptable than some less-than-inspired translation into English. Perhaps I should add that I enjoy all aspects of food and that we have over 80 cookery books on our kitchen bookshelf!

There are dangers when using a dictionary. The translation may be correct in itself but there may be a proprietary or trade name that is more appropriate. For example, most mechanically-minded people call a hexagonal socket key an 'allen key', or a cross-point screwdriver a 'Philips screwdriver'. The same pitfalls occur in foreign languages of course. A dictionary is used more as an aide memoire and really all you want is confirmation of what you're looking for. A couple of examples serve to illustrate the insecurity of relying on dictionaries:

- Swedish entry: *pay-back metoden*, English translation: *pay-off-period method*
- Swedish entry: *kronofogde*, English translation: *County Division Police Commissioner*. However, in a supplement to the same dictionary which is all the same volume, a different translation is given: *Head of Enforcement District*.

As technology advances, more and more on-line dictionaries and encyclopaedias are becoming available. These can be consulted at any time while you are still working in your word processor program and are available on CD-ROM disks purely because of the sheer volume of storage required.

I use these regularly since they can be used to drop text directly into your translation and provide an excellent complement to what you can build up in terminology management systems such as MultiTerm.

6.2   Standards

An extremely useful source of terminology is found in standards. By standards I mean documents produced by bodies such as the British Standards Institution (BSI), the International Standards Organisation (ISO) and others. These bodies issue standards on a whole range of subjects – usually technical. There is a hierarchy of standards with ISO and other international bodies at the top. National standards are usually harmonised with international standards and form the next level. Large companies often publish their own standards which, in turn, tend to be in harmony with national standards. A typical example, shown on the next page, is reproduced with the kind permission of Volvo's Standards Department, Gothenburg, Sweden.

Many of these standards contain terms in several languages. Swedish standards, for example, are often available in several languages and provide excellent sources of reference. In most cases, the original language term is listed with a brief explanation. This is then followed by the term translated into at least one other foreign language – usually English.

BSI is the UK agent for all international standards. It has a sales office where standards can be purchased. (See Appendix for details). Large libraries have copies of British Standards. There is even a British Standard on the presentation of translations (Ref. 8). Its full title is 'Specification for the presentation of translations' BS 4755:1971.

6.3   Research Institutes and Professional/ Trade Association Libraries

Assume that you have a translation on building services (the bits and pieces inside a building such as heating, ventilating, sanitation). Obviously a useful source of information would be the library of the appropriate research association – The Building Services Research and Information Association in this case. Normally their services are available only to members but some help is offered to non-members.

There is a reference book available listing all the relevant associations. It is entitled 'Directory of British Associations & Associations in Ireland'. Further details are given in the references in the appendix to this book.

6.4   Past translations

It would be ideal if you could save all past hard-copy translations and reference material. There is however a limit to how much of this material you can physically store. Likewise, you will need an efficient retrieval system if it is going to be of any use. Your translations can be stored on disk rather than as hard copy. The amount of text that can be stored on magnetic media is considerable. It can also be retrieved rapidly when the need arises if you are disciplined in cataloguing your computer files.

Obviously the use of translation memory systems greatly facilitates this operation. More so MultiTerm than Translator's Workbench since most of your research work will be done on terminology. This represents a considerable asset and should be stored securely since just one term may take several hours and phone calls to resolve.

6.4.1   Detective work

One of the most interesting and, at the same time, most demanding translation assignments I have had in my career was to translate the web site of a Swedish forestry company. This demanded not only my translation skills but also what might be termed life experience skills covering the following:

Understanding and being able to translate recipes

This was necessary since the website talked about what game animals, bird and fish could be hunted in the forest. This required not only an understanding of and feel for cooking so that the recipe would work when translated but also knowing what to call the translated recipe. My mother encouraged me from an early age to cook and this has become a lifelong pleasure. I used Swedish, English and French references from a selection of the 100 or more cookery books that I've collected to date.

It would be nice to work through the recipes although getting hold of ingredients such as 3 kg of steak from the hind leg of a bear could be a tad difficult.

Knowing the names of freshwater fish – both game and coarse

This was a challenge since one particular fish (*Sik*, sometimes called whitefish in English) has six different varieties in Sweden only some of which are to be found in British waters – the gwyniad and pouting. The only solution in some cases is to revert to the Latin name or use this as a common denominator for further research.

Having a knowledge of Sweden's climate, geography, geology, flora and fauna in general

Again, the names of different flora can be difficult especially if the species are restricted to distinct geographical areas. Thanks to Carl von Linné (Linnaeus to most people, and a Swede don't you know, 1707–1778) there are the Latin common denominators that be used to assist the hapless translator.

Knowing where to look if you can't find the term in your standard reference works

For this translation I used 17 reference books in addition to the standard bilingual dictionaries. This often required quite a bit of detective work that may seem out of all proportion for just one word.

This particular word occurred in connection with the history of one of Sweden's largest lakes, Storsjön, in the county of Jämtland. There is an island on this lake and, in 1689, a property was purchased on the island to provide a *regementsskrivarboställe*. It was this particular term that required some degree of detective work and the flowchart below shows the path that led to the translation of the word that I made.

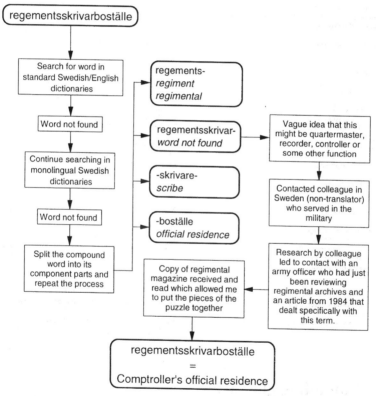

I decided on the use of comptroller after checking for the word's definition in the New Oxford Dictionary of English. From the Swedish article I found that the title *regementsskrivaren* was in use between 1646 and 1880 when it was changed to *regementsintendent*. The latter can be translated as *regimental paymaster*.

VOLVO
KONCERNSTANDARD
GROUP STANDARDS

STD 5023,61

| Handläggare Issued by | 06530 L-G Olsson | Utgåva Issue | 1 | Fastställd Established | 1987-05 | Sida Page | 1 (3) |

RITNINGSREGLER
KRAV FÖR MIKROFILMNING

TECHNICAL DRAWINGS
REQUIREMENTS FOR MICROCOPYING

ORIENTERING

Denna standard är ett utdrag ur den internationella standarden ISO 6428-1982 och den svenska standarden SS-ISO 6428.

Standarden ersätter STD 5021,51

ORIENTATION

This standard consists of an extract from the international standard ISO 6428-1982 and the Swedish standard SS-ISO 6428.

The standard replaces STD 5021,51

INNEHÅLL

1 ALLMÄNT

2 KRAV PÅ UTFÖRANDE
2.1 Ritningsblanketter
2.2 Linjer, svärtning, linjegrovlek och linjeavstånd
2.3 Ytor
2.4 Markeringar
2.5 Textning
2.6 Rithjälpmedel

3 REFERENSER

CONTENTS

1 GENERAL

2 REQUIREMENTS OF EXECUTION
2.1 Drawing sheets
2.2 Density, thickness and spacing of lines
2.3 Areas
2.4 Markings
2.5 Lettering
2.6 Equipment for drawing

3 REFERENCES

1 ALLMÄNT

Denna standard anger de krav som skall iakttas när man upprättar originalritningar och andra dokument som skall mikrofilmas. Uppfyllda krav ger mikrofilm av hög kvalitet av vilken läsbara, förstorade kopior kan göras.

Reglerna kan emellertid med stor fördel tillämpas för andra reprometoder. Därför rekommenderas det att alla dokument upprättas enligt denna standard, så att de kan användas för framtida mikrofilmning.

1 GENERAL

This standard specifies the requirements to be observed when executing original technical drawings and other drawing office documents which are to be microcopied. These requirements will provide for high quality microforms with which legible enlargement copies can be made.

However, the application of these rules is also very beneficial to other methods of reproduction and it is therefore recommended that all drawing office documents be executed in accordance with this standard, thereby being available for microcopying at a future date.

6.5 Compiling glossaries

A useful approach to adopt when faced with new subject matter is to compile a glossary before you start the translation proper. Check what is already available before 're-inventing the wheel'. Scan through the source document for unfamiliar words and make a list of them. You can use your computer for this.

Let's look at a very simple example taken from a translation on newspaper handling machinery. The words are taken in the order they appear in the text.

Swedish	English
öppningsvred	opening handle
LCD-kort	LCD card
gränslägesbrytare	limit switch
blinka	flash
hissanordning	lifting gear
hyllplan	storage plate
minusknappen	minus button
parametervärde	parameter value

Your way of compiling your own glossaries can be as simple or as complex as you wish to make it. Probably the simplest way is to use the sort facility in the word processing program that you are using. While this has the advantage of simplicity it does not usually allow simple electronic retrieval. If you are familiar with translation memory systems then the use of terminology management software is preferable since it allows you to search to see whether you have already stored the word or term and drop it into your document.

A glossary is of course much simpler to use if it is in alphabetical order so get the computer to do the work. Just make a final check to ensure that words beginning with å, ä, ö, etc are placed in the correct order. The only disadvantage of using this method is that some word processing programs do not allow you to swap columns. This can be an advantage if you decide you want to have a list with English as the source language. You can of course sort on the second column but this means looking at the second column first.

Swedish	English
blinka	flash
gränslägesbrytare	limit switch
hissanordning	lifting gear
hyllplan	storage plate
LCD-kort	LCD card
minusknappen	minus button
parametervärde	parameter value
öppningsvred	opening handle

You can now use your list as a reference while you are translating. You also have a permanent record for future use. A further advantage is that you can submit your glossary to your client for possible checking or harmonisation with existing terminology. When approved, you can include it in your translation software terminology bank with reference to the client as the source.

Lists such as this are very useful if you store a particular client's translations on special disks. A client may have a preferred term for a specific application even though there are other options that are equally valid. How do you remember which term a particular client uses if you do not have a record to which you can refer? You may need to wait for a year or so between assignments so ease of access to previous translations is important.

Ideally a translation should be done by a single translator if only to retain the same style throughout. A further risk, when a translation is split between several translators, is the lack of harmonisation on terminology. There are times when a translation project is so large that it is beyond the capacity of a single translator. It then becomes necessary to appoint one person who has overall responsibility for harmonisation. The use of computer-aided translation and electronic terminology management can facilitate this task. Agreed translations of terminology items can be inserted before the translation is sent to the different members of the translation team. This will ensure consistency of usage.

I have been fortunate in having worked on major projects with other translators and where I have taken the initiative to compile a glossary of terms. Naturally, such a glossary starts from humble beginnings and grows as other members of the translation team add their contributions. The glossary is updated on a regular basis, say once a week, and is distributed to those working on the project. This ensures that 'standard' terminology is used. To give an example, a glossary that resulted from a project on which I worked for around two years ended up by running into well over 60 pages and has been adopted as a company reference source.

Terminology management systems such as MultiTerm allow you to store your glossaries for re-use. But a word of caution! Make sure your glossary terms in MultiTerm and translated segments in Translators Workbench are correct before committing them to your computer memory otherwise you will perpetuate any mistakes.

6.6　Product literature

Product literature in the target language is a useful source of terminology. The dilemma is deciding what to collect, how to store it and, not least, how to retrieve it when you need it. Since time is always at a premium, it is hardly ever practical to try and get hold of additional reference literature from outside sources when you have a translation in progress.

It is probably best to store your reference material according to subject matter. You can store your glossaries in the same place. If you work for a limited number of clients, you may find it more convenient to store the material accordingly. Papers and leaflets do not stand neatly in a bookshelf and there is nothing worse than untidy papers lying around. Either file the relevant papers in ring binders or use box files that stand up on their own on your bookshelf. I use sturdy plastic box files and attach labels to the spine to identify contents.

6.7 Data retrieval and file management

File management for individual freelance translators

Before you start saving text files on disk, consider that you may need to retrieve information some time in the future. If you have called the file something very simple such as 'TRANS123' it is going to be very difficult at some later date to retrieve a translation that was done for a particular client.

A certain level of bureaucracy is inevitable but can be very useful. Most computer files can be named with alphanumeric characters and a three-character extension. Punctuation is not usually permitted. This is changing as newer versions of software are released. In fact, only certain extensions are recognised by some software. You will need to devise a system that you feel at home with, but some guidance could be useful. The characters permitted when identifying files vary according to the software package you use. Some packages provide the option of annotating file statistics, extended file names, author details etc. Consult your manual to find out what is available.

A system that is simple to use if you translate into only one target language is as follows. Use four numeric characters for the sequential job number – 1224 for example, an underscore character _, three letters to denote source language, three to denote target language and a three-character extension to denote the software format (a Microsoft Word document in this example). Thus the job number appears as follows:

1224_swe_eng.doc

Rather than billing for each individual assignment I bill regular clients at the end of each month for all work done during that month. Once all work is signed off for that month the sub-directory for the month (and all its files) are transferred to the ARCHIVE directory. Consequently only work in progress for a particular month is stored in the LIVE directory. Work for occasional customers is filed in the same way but invoicing is done when the work is delivered.

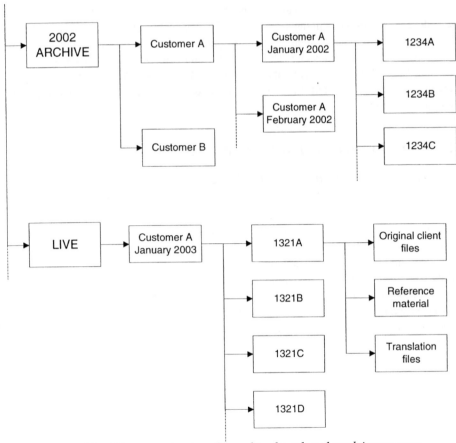

Figure 12. Directory structure for archived work and work in progress

File management for translation companies

The above system is quite adequate when dealing with single language pairs on a stand-alone system used by an individual translator. A translation company running a network of several computers needs a system that can cope with a range of language pairs and translations at various stages of production.

If a job comprises a significant number of individual files I find it useful to compile an Excel file to keep track of progress. An example of a job containing a large number of files is shown on page 90. The last line can be used for formulae to indicate the state of work in progress.

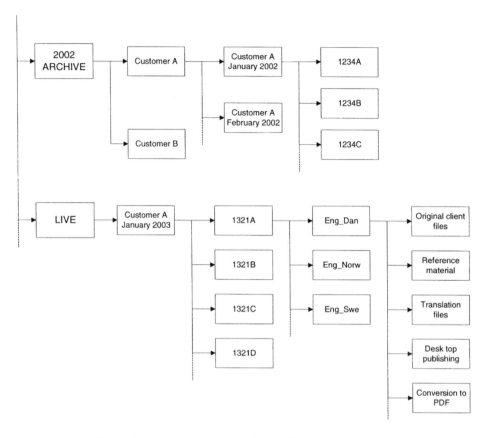

Figure 13. File management for multiple language pairs

6.8 Database applications

There is a danger when working with a computer. You can get hooked on using it for its own sake rather than its serving you and lightening your administrative burden. There are applications where the use of a database program is enormously time-saving – I could say indispensable but people did manage before computers. Card indexes are easily accessible if they hold a small amount of data but cards can get lost. A computer index can be readily updated or amended and you can structure your data to provide precisely the format in which you wish to view it. It is also impractical to try to analyse data on a card index when you consider the agility that a computer offers.

A PRACTICAL GUIDE FOR TRANSLATORS

September 9, 2002   Job No.1282 – TRANSLATION FILE RECORD

Filename	Words	Trans-lated	1st proof	2nd proof	Spell-check	Final read	Date delivered
S2.doc	70	70	70	70	X	X	09-Sep-02
S5-7_inled.doc	353	353	353	353	X	X	09-Sep-02
S8-10_Forord.doc	608	608	608	608	X	X	09-Sep-02
s12-18_Bakgrund.doc	1286	1286	1286	1286	X	X	09-Sep-02
S20-21_Gripenkonceptet	275	275	275	275	X	X	09-Sep-02
s22-27_Flygplanet.doc	529	529	529	529	X	X	09-Sep-02
s28-31_Gripensysteemet.doc	973	973	973	973	X	X	09-Sep-02
s32-35_Bev_o_yttre_laster.doc	588	588	588	588	X	X	09-Sep-02
s36-42_Manniskan_i_Gripens.doc	1119	1119	1119	1119	X	X	09-Sep-02
s44-48_Ekonomi.doc	1063	1063	1063	1063	X	X	09-Sep-02
s50-54_Kontrakten.doc	880	880	880	880	X	X	09-Sep-02
s56-58_Partners_och.doc	486	486	486	486	X	X	09-Sep-02
s60-61_Exportstod.doc	381	381	381	381	X	X	09-Sep-02
s62-65_Saab_BAE.doc	605	605	605	605	X	X	09-Sep-02
s66-69_Exportsatsn.doc	665	665	665	665	X	X	09-Sep-02
s70-72_Vidareutv_av_Gr.doc	423	423	423	423	X	X	09-Sep-02
s74-75_Gripen_dorroppn.doc	407	407	407	407	X	X	09-Sep-02
s78-81_Utvecklingspot.doc	588	588	588	588	X	X	09-Sep-02
s82-85_JAS_39_Gripen_-_.doc	626	626	626	626	X	X	09-Sep-02
s86-88_JAS_39_Gripen_i_f.doc	705	705	705	705	X	X	09-Sep-02
s90-92_Flygvapnets_utb.doc	430	430	430	430	X	X	09-Sep-02
s94-95_Pilotens_syn.doc	299	299	299	299	X	X	09-Sep-02
s96-97_Teknik_pa_framk.doc	367	367	367	367	X	X	09-Sep-02
s98-99_Tekn_tjanst_pa.doc	278	278	278	278	X	X	09-Sep-02
s100-102_Pilotens_utrustn.doc	676	676	676	676	X	X	09-Sep-02
s104-106_Internationella_op.doc	644	644	644	644	X	X	09-Sep-02
s108-110_Fjarde_gen.doc	380	380	380	380	X	X	09-Sep-02
s112-115_Darfor_valde_Sydaf.doc	553	553	553	553	X	X	09-Sep-02
s116-118_Darfor_valde_Ung.doc	414	414	414	414	X	X	09-Sep-02
s120-127_Nationella_op.doc	1605	1605	1605	1605	X	X	09-Sep-02
s130-136_Historien.doc	1347	1347	1347	1347	X	X	09-Sep-02
s154-165_Gripen_nagra_mil.doc	1567	1567	1567	1567	X	X	09-Sep-02
s176_forfattarna.doc	83	83	83	83	X	X	09-Sep-02
Totals	21273	21273	21273	21273			
Left to translate/proof-read/spell-check		0	0	0			

Compilation of glossaries and term lists

Depending on the software you use, there are two levels of glossaries and term lists – those generated when using pure text process programs such as Microsoft Word and those generated in terminology management systems associated with CAT programs such as MultiTerm referred to earlier.

In essence, a database comprises a number of records each made up of fields (alpha-numeric, date, numeric, logic, memo). Once you have entered your data you can then structure your records according to the criteria you specify.

You can decide which language is to be the source language and the equivalent terms will then be put in the correct order so that they follow the alphabetically-indexed source language. A report can be structured so that the terms are printed in columns with a suitable heading for each column plus a heading for each page. Records can be sorted using the facilities provided in standard word processing packages but as the number of parameters increases a database program becomes more practical.

Keeping a production record

A production record on computer can be used for a number of applications. You can use it to analyse your production over a given period. You can use the data to keep track of when you received or delivered a particular job. It allows you to trace past jobs so that you can quickly retrieve a job that you may have done a couple of years back.

Field names are usually limited to around 10 characters and you determine the type of field and the number of characters it contains when you set up the database. If, as in the case of SOURCE (source language), you set the field length to 3 characters, the computer will automatically go to the next field as soon as the present field is full. WORDS is a numeric field and will allow you to total the fields for a specific range of records. Date fields such as DATEDEL (date delivered) will allow you to calculate the number of words you produced over a specific period. You may have differentiated charge rates – these can also be specified.

DATE fields allow you to extract data according to specific date criteria. NUMERIC fields allow you to carry out simple mathematical operations on the data contained in the respective fields. You could, for example, ask your computer to total the number of words you have translated for a particular client between 1 January and 30 June. You can make the database as complex as you wish but make sure it serves you as a tool and is not full of data for which you have no real practical use.

Maintaining an address list

Address lists of clients and suppliers (and freelances if you progress to running your own translation company) can be easily compiled and updated. In theory, at least, once you have all the details entered, you can use the list for a variety of purposes.

Memo fields are not usually displayed and can be used to note any confidential details about a client. The client may require specific layouts or procedures, he may be a slow payer, you may wish to add specific notes about the company, and so on.

Address labels can be readily printed from the database. This is useful when updating clients with information about your business (or when sending Christmas cards). Likewise you can structure your indexed data to provide an alphabetical list of clients with their associated reference numbers or a numerical list of clients and the respective names.

Reference/trade literature and past translations

Remembering all the reference literature you have carefully filed away is almost impossible. If you do make the effort to list this in a database, it will facilitate the task of retrieval. You can also print out a list of what you've got for ready reference. The same can be applied to past translations. There may be a considerable gap between receiving translation assignments on a particular subject. It is therefore gratifying to be able to retrieve information without difficulty.

7 Quality control and accountability

'All the goodness of a good egg cannot make up for the badness of a bad one.'
Charles Anderson Dana, 1819–1897

Your reputation as a translator will be determined by the quality of the translations you produce. The question is, 'Who or what determines an acceptable level of quality?'. The quality of a tangible object such as a metal bolt can be checked against a well-defined standard and such assessment can be fairly objective. A translation is, however, an intangible entity and quality can be very subjective in many cases and control is a fairly mechanical process. There are certain guidelines which can be applied and which rectify obvious errors.

The mere fact that you are a competent translator must be tempered by the realisation that you have your limitations. Subject knowledge is essential. A client is not likely to be happy if you accept an assignment and then produce a poor quality translation – even though you may have done your level best with the resources you have available.

Ideally you should have your work checked by a colleague. This is however seldom practical, particularly if you are working in isolation. The luxury of checking is afforded only to people who work in a group or in partnership. Checking your own work is very difficult – you see what you want to see. By giving your translation to an independent checker you get the translation checked more objectively. You can of course reject the checker's comment or come to a consensus.

7.1 Source text difficulties

Source text difficulties are many but the two most common are linguistic content and its layout.

As a translator you need to understand the source text – this is a fundamental requirement. But what happens if the source text is poorly written, ambiguous or contains words that are used inappropriately? My attitude may appear arrogant but there are cases where I have sent back a source text and asked for it to be revised so it makes sense – not because I do not understand the language I am translating from but because the way it is written makes it impossible to translate with confidence. Rather than being undiplomatic I highlight the text that does not make sense and ask for its meaning to be explained so that a proper translation can be made. Inevitably there are the time constraints that all translators are familiar with but that is the nature of the profession unless radical changes take place.

The layout of the source text often causes problems particularly is the person who keyed in the text does not make use of style sheets and used the spacebar to format a document. A further problem arises, often in annual reports, where the source text is written in a spreadsheet program such as Excel. Text occupies a cell of a finite length and may continue in several cells. Inevitably the translated text will expand and cannot be accommodated in the space available. Consequently some words need to be carried over into the next cell and results in a domino effect. There may also be hidden macros in the spreadsheet that will not permit translation without the links in the spreadsheet being violated.

These are some of the many issues to be considered before accepting a translation assignment. It is all too easy to blame the result on the translator so it is our responsibility to ensure that what we work with allows us to exercise our skills appropriately and safeguard our status as professionals.

7.2 Translation quality in relation to purpose, price and urgency

Apart from your skills and competence, there are three significant factors that determine the quality of a translation. Perhaps the most important factor to consider when producing a translation is what it is going to be used for.

The principal applications for translation are:

- Information
- Text scanning and abstracting
- Publication
- Legal
- Notarisation or certification.

Some of these do of course overlap. Let's look at the different applications in turn and consider the levels of quality control required.

7.2.1 Translation used for information

In this case, the end reader must be able to understand the content of the original and for the translation to contain an accurate reflection of the facts and figures it contains. The client may even specify that the result does not have to be a complete translation since the intended reader may only be interested in certain facts. You may even be asked just to summarise the important elements of the text in a few pages. Let me give a couple of examples.

A company may be considering a takeover of another company and will want to know all the essential financial data about the target of the takeover bid. Time is usually very tight in such cases, particularly if other companies may be competing for the takeover. It is quite likely that the information they have will contain a lot of irrelevant detail. Consequently, it is the task of the translator to scan through the text and pick out all the information of importance.

We recently received a fax from one of our clients late on a Friday evening for delivery on the following Monday morning. It contained 101 pages! The original information contained lots of marketing and sales information and the brief from the client was, 'Pick out what you think could be of interest to us and translate it!' The end result was 10 pages of information. Perhaps I should add that we had already done a lot of work on the same project so we had a good idea of what they were looking for. We delivered a draft translation on the following Monday morning. Since this translation was needed just for information and so urgently, the quality controls carried out were: spell checking, grammar checking and a check of all the figures. These were all done by the same translator.

It is difficult in a case like this for a checker to exercise any major degree of quality control – time does not allow for this. He would almost need to duplicate the work of the first translator. Naturally, a premium was charged for working over the weekend to complete this assignment on time. The time taken to read through all the 101 pages to extract the necessary information was also considered in the charge.

Another example may be an invitation to tender. Naturally, a client does not want or need to have a complete document translated so that he can pick out one or two pieces of important information. The client may decide as a result of your scanning the information that he is not interested in submitting a bid or that the deadline for replies does not allow him to do the necessary calculations. Quite often you may need to sit in a client's office and scan through the documentation and provide a verbal translation, possibly dictated, on site for the client. In such cases, your own competence is the only thing you can rely on and quality control to any great extent is provided only when the client asks questions. The client needs to be made aware of the level of accuracy you can achieve under such circumstances.

7.2.2   Text scanning and abstracting

There are occasions when a client may not wish to have a complete document translated for the simple reason that most of it may not be relevant. It is useful to the client if you are able to scan mentally through the document and extract the information required. It may be necessary to translate certain parts in full but you will have saved your client time as well as money. Administrative or legal details can be sorted out while the 'meat' of the proposal is being prepared.

Abstracting is a particular skill. It means gleaning details from a document and providing salient information (in translated form) in a fixed number of words. Several industries produce journals containing abstracts. By reading such journals, people are able to read the important points and determine whether a complete translation is warranted.

The amount of information that some people are required to read as part of their job is quite considerable in some cases. Consequently, it is useful if the person concerned is given a summary or abstract of an article to read. The reader can then decide whether the article is relevant to his or her work, and whether a complete translation would be worthwhile. Abstracts in technical journals usually amount to around 100 words. This demands considerable editorial skill on the part of the translator. Quality in this case is being able to extract the information that is of real use to the client. Of course, the standard spell checking and grammar checking are expected. The following pages show an original article and the resulting abstract.

7.2.3   Translating a complete text for information

Most translations produced for information purposes are complete translations. The translation needs to be completely accurate in terms of facts and figures. The aesthetic quality of the language is less important but should nevertheless be taken into consideration. The minimum quality controls carried out in this case are:

- Resolve any queries that you may have with a subject expert or the client.
- Check to ensure that all the text has been translated. This may sound elementary but you can easily be disturbed for a number of reasons and miss a word, line, paragraph or even page.
- Check all the figures and dates in the text and in tables.
- Carry out a spell check using your word processor program and grammar check if this facility is available.
- Pass the translation to a colleague for checking. He will be able to take a more objective view of the translation, and will duplicate the checks you have made.
- Discuss any corrections with the checker, where required. The checker will have the same language capabilities as yourself but perhaps not the same level of ability or experience. Incorporate the corrections and changes where these are relevant. Repeat the spell check to ensure that the corrections and changes do not contain typing errors.

Building simulation and building representation: Overview of current developments

A J Wright† MSc PhD MCIBSE, **D Bloomfield**‡ BSc MCIBSE and **T J Wiltshire**† BSc PhD MCIBSE
† School of Architecture, University of Newcastle upon Tyne, Newcastle upon Tyne NE1 7RU, UK
‡ Systems Performance Prediction Section, Building Research Establishment, Garston, Watford WD2 7JR, UK

Received 22 April 1991, in final form 5 August 1991

1 Introduction

It would be an enormous and pointless task to carry out a thorough review of all the thermal building programs currently available. Many studies comparing programs have already been carried out[1,2] comparing their performance for the same problem with each other, and with measured data, and reviewing their capabilities.

The purpose of this paper is to take an overview of the current state of thermal modelling, and to look at trends for the future. It is shown how in the short term, the data structures of current programs combined with forces driving program development tend to hinder improvements to building simulation, while in the longer term, the emergence of new tools offers hope for the future.

A major focus of current research in the engineering and construction industries reviewed here is data modelling and the development of an international standard for the exchange of product data (STEP). For buildings, the aim is to have a general schema for describing any building, in order to facilitate the exchange of information between different members of the design team. If this is successful, this would clearly have implications for simulation programs; those conforming to the standard would obviously be favoured by the industry, and integration of design tools would be greatly eased. At present, the language and structure for STEP have been defined but standard sets of entities in specific application areas remain largely undefined. There is currently no agreed data model for a building.

In computing, object oriented programming (OOP) is rapidly becoming established as a powerful and highly productive approach to many areas of programming, as the hardware to support it becomes widely available and inexpensive. Because this technique brings a high degree of modularity to data structures and functions by encapsulating both within software objects which map to real-world objects, it is claimed to be the best available method for producing programs sharing such objects, and also maps closely onto the real-world objects of a data model such as STEP; the language of STEP, Express has several object-oriented features. Four current projects using OOP to produce flexible environments for building simulation, each with a different emphasis, are described here.

2 Structures of current programs

It is necessary to consider the structures of current simulation programs before trying to find a solution to the problems which arise. The relationships between the user and different knowledge sources during the thermal modelling process are shown in Figure 1, from Reference 2, for a generalised plant and control modelling system. (In reality, no single system would offer a wide choice at the Knowledge Base level, and in many cases only one solver would be available.) The situation is very similar when modelling buildings. Clearly, there are a number of different data representations at different stages.

Figure 2 shows the different stages of simulation typical of the current generation of programs. A user defines the problem for the program, using databases both directly and indirectly within the computer. At each timestep, the description of the problem within the computer is then used to form the coefficients for the systems of equations which model the physical processes, and a set of boundary conditions. These equations are solved by a numerical process to give a set of calculated results which are stored as output; some results are also fed back into the system of equations to be used at the next timestep.

The inner box in Figure 2 contains the calculation loop carried out at each time step. The different forms of data representation are now described in more detail for building the 1989 Fundamentals, such as earlier versions of the Handbook. Solutions are included for over 90% of the problems. The solutions are generally presented in abbreviated form, with some of the in-between numerical computations omitted.

NOx emission control for gas turbines - a 1991 update on regulations and technology

Schorr M M.   92-00359

Energy Engng. 1991, vol.88, no.6, 25-54, 9 figs, 3 refs.

Discusses the current legislative and regulatory emission control requirements in the USA, including the new Clean Air Act Amendments, and the technologies that are currently available to control pollutant emissions from gas turbines.

Optimising heat recovery from combustion exhaust gases. (in Italian)

Sergio A. et al   92-00360

Termotecnica January 1992, no.1, 61-66, 4 figs, 6 refs.

States that heat recovery from combustion exhaust gases can be correlated with the efficiency of the exchanger or of the regenerator in order to define the maximum yield as a function of the optimum surface. Describes a calculation algorithm developed for the personal computer, which makes it possible to determine the thermal optimum for different operating conditions, and to make comparisons between alternative solutions.

The utilisation and optimisation of a building's thermal inertia in minimising the overall energy use

Simmonds P.   92-00361

ASHRAE Trans. 1991, vol.97, part 2, paper number IN-91-16-4, 1031-1042, 12 figs, 5 tabs, refs

Shows how the optimal design of the heating and ventilating plant of an office building was achieved by utilising the building's thermal inertia for both winter and summer operations using dynamic computer simulation programs.

Design and evaluation of a fast-burn spark-ignition combustion system for gaseous fuels at high compression ratios

Stone C R., Ladommatos N.   92-00362

J.Inst.Energy December 1991, 202-211, 7 figs, 3 tabs, 34 refs.

States that the use of cogeneration has led to strong interest in converting diesel engines to spark-ignition operation on gaseous fuels. Reviews the two combustion-system options (open chamber and pre-combustion chamber) and presents the advantages of an open-chamber combustion system. Discusses the design philosophy of a fast-burn high-compression-ratio lean-burn combustion system, and presents experimental values from tests using natural gas and natural gas/carbon dioxide mixtures. Places particular emphasis on the combustion analysis and emissions performance and notes that considerable potential has been demonstrated for low specific emissions of nitrogen oxides. Presents comprehensive performance data for equivalence ratios in the range of 0.5 to 1.2 for the engine operating at 1500 rev min with a wide-open throttle.

Building simulation and building representation - overview of current developments

Wright A J.   92-00363

Bldg.Serv.Engng.Res.Tech. 1992, vol.13, no.1, 1-11, 4 figs, 31 refs.

Reviews the current state of thermal modelling for buildings, and describes developments in data modelling, object-oriented programming and specific research projects which indicate the likely course of future developments. Describes the limitations of the data structures plus processes of current programs, in the context of the forces which drive development. Examines from the viewpoint of building modelling emerging international data exchange standards, which are likely to be a major influence on future engineering software. Explains the applicability of object-oriented programming to building simulation. Finally, describes a number of research projects, some of which aim to facilitate the production of new simulation programs, while others aim to integrate a set of design tools sharing a common building description.

Heat pumps and heat recovery

Rating of mixed, split, residential heat pumps operating in the heating mode

Domanski P A.   92-00364

ASHRAE Trans. 1991, vol.97, part 2, paper number 3525, 324-330, 4 figs, 2 tabs, refs

Presents an analysis and methodology for rating the performance of mixed, single-speed, split, residential heat pumps operating in the heating mode. States the method allows for calculation of the capacity at the DOE 8.3°C (47°F) rating point and the heating seasonal performance factor for the minimum design heating requirement in Region 4 without performing laboratory testing of a complete system. The analysis includes evaluation of the impact of the indoor coil, expansion device and fan on system performance. Also discusses verification and applicability limits of the procedure.

Solar-assisted heat pump systems - assessment of an example using profiled steel cladding

Loveday D L.   92-00365

Bldg.Serv.Res.Tech. 1992, vol.13, no.1, 37-41, 4 figs, 3 tabs, 18 refs.

Presents correlation equations which describe the in situ performance of an air-source heat pump installed in a UK house. The equations are used for assessing the effect on overall system performance of heat pump solar assistance provided by profiled steel cladding acting as an air preheater. Compares the results with those for the cases of conventional tile roof preheating and no preheating at all, and validates the assessment procedure with reference to measured data for the tile roof case. Shows that the system performance can be enhanced by use of the cladding. However, the effects of fan power and defrost cycling are shown to be important, and concludes that a full investigation of the cost effectiveness of such a system is warranted before application on a large scale.

You need to be aware that major decisions may be made on the basis of the information you provide in your translation, so there is no room for complacency or carelessness in your work. You can, however, safely say that the end result does not need to be a literary masterpiece although the language should of course be correct.

7.2.4 Translations for publication

This is where the work of the translator starts to get more serious. The translation may be published as a company document read by a restricted number of people, or it may constitute the basis of a very expensive colour publication. What you need to consider in this case is that a considerable amount of additional work will be done on your translation before the publication reaches its intended reader. If your translation turns out to be of an unacceptable quality, you may be liable for the cost of all the additional work done subsequent to your translation. The fact that your translation costs only 15% of the total production cost is of no significance.

One thing you should be aware of is that you are not responsible for any additions or errors made to the text made by the client after you have finished your work on it. Ideally, you should have the opportunity of seeing the final version of the text before it is printed.

7.2.5 Translations used in advertising and marketing

Producing advertising copy is an art in itself and should really be kept apart from translation. Ideally, the translator should produce the most faithful rendering of the text possible, while being allowed due editorial licence, and then hand over the copy to a copywriter or editor. The end result may be perfectly correct but may be 'the wrong colour'. Notes will probably be needed to explain why a certain concept won't work in its translated form. This is something you need to discuss with the client before accepting an assignment.

The client will, in all probability, have invested considerable resources in producing the final version of the text in the source language. Is it therefore not right that sufficient resources be devoted to producing advertising copy in a foreign language?

Ideally, the text should be sent to the client's agent or subsidiary in the country where the language is spoken. What sells in England won't necessarily sell in Germany for example. Similarly, the methods used for marketing in one country may not be applicable to another country.

Get a detailed specification from the client

You can only do what the client asks for. So get all the necessary details in writing. It's no use referring to an obscure telephone conversation when the project has gone off the rails. After all, quality is providing what the client has asked for and, if this is not documented, your argument is severely weakened. Consider the following points before starting a translation:

- What type of publication is the translation going to be used in?
- What style of text is required – how much editorial licence is allowed or required?
- Is a copywriter going to work on the text?
- Does the translation need to be fitted into a given space. Remember, a translation will not produce the same number of words as the original text.
- What is the client going to do with the translation?
- Who is going to be responsible for verifying the translation?

Many translators are unaware of all the additional work that is done once they have sent the translation to a client. The level of feedback to the translator is often low or non-existent. It is usually when the translation is poor or exceptionally good that any comment is heard.

7.2.6 Producing a translation that will be used to make further translations

There are many occasions when translations into English are subsequently translated into other languages. In such cases, the translator must bear in mind that the second translator must not be faced with ambiguities that did not exist to the original text. As in all cases, the quality of the translation is determined by the quality of the source language. This is sometimes called the GIGO factor – Garbage In, Garbage Out!

SUPPORT

Prediction for financial support can only be identified in the short term.

As previously researched potential is greater than originally indicated.

How far and how fast would an investor wish XYZ Limited to develop?

How much corporate support is available via an investor?

These factors will influence current and future requirements.

To create an independent operation utilizing established support services, with the perceived status congruent to major blue-chip corporations potentially approachable would require a minimum investment of £100,000 – £150,000.

Planned growth could be organic or funded and therefore accelerated.

The above must be open to negotiation and discussion.

Figure 15. An example of garbage text

The above is a good example of the need for pre-translation editing. The original author may have been quite clear in his mind about what he is trying to say. But, with the best will in the world, you as the translator may have great difficulty in understanding what the author intended. In many cases, the author will not have read through the text after having written it and will seldom, if ever, write with the translator in mind. In case of any doubt, ask the client. The example shows the need to edit the source text prior to translating it. This is not a fictitious example. It was part of a report submitted to a venture capitalist in an endeavour to raise funds! I'll leave it to you to try and make sense of the text.

7.3   Localisation

The quality of your translation may be perfectly adequate, but the style and presentation may not suit the intended market. The best results we achieve are produced by working together with the client's offices abroad so that they add their comments on the translation before the final version is submitted to the client.

This can be very useful since those working in the country where the language is spoken are aware of current language usage and any appropriate jargon. This is particularly important in marketing. A brand name that is perfectly acceptable in one country may sound ridiculous in another. (Mitsubishi 'Pajero', Swedish 'Plopp' chocolate etc). I'm sure you have come across a number of examples.

7.4   Translations for legal purposes

This is where the work of the translator really starts to get serious. The position of a comma in a sentence could change the verdict.

An example in Swedish is:

BENÅDAS, EJ DEPORTERAS (To be reprieved, not deported)
or
BENÅDAS EJ, DEPORTERAS (Not to be reprieved, to be deported)

Translating a legal text is not easy. Just to give an example, I once took a class of Swedish law students where we discussed a translation of a text on 'General terms governing bank loans' issued by a major Swedish bank. The law students were unable to agree on the interpretation of some of the clauses in the original Swedish let alone attempt a confident translation. The message is not to consider legal translations lightly. There are concepts in law which may exist in one country yet not in another. What does the translator do in this case?

Footnotes are often preferable to translator's notes at the end of the text. Footnotes make immediate reference to the item in question and draw the reader's attention to the fact straight away.

If your translation is going to be used as evidence in a court of law you must consider the responsibility you have. In all probability the translation will have to be notarised. In a few cases, a notary public may have a knowledge of the language you have translated and can actually check that your translation is correct. Others merely witness a written statement that you have made and affix their seal. The level of quality control required is very high and your charges should reflect the cost of the additional checking work that must be done.

If your legal translation is made for information purposes only, you should add a statement at the end of your work in line with the following.

'Although due care and attention has been given to this translation, it should not be considered a legal document and the original language document takes precedence over this translation in any dispute over interpretation'.

Apart from making the standard checks, you need to be able to say, hand on heart, 'Is this translation as accurate as I can make it?'. You will come across legal concepts that may not exist in the target language, and a literal translation will be entirely unacceptable. You must be able to understand fully the implications of what is said in the source language and produce the nearest accepted equivalent in the target language.

This type of translation may demand translator's notes. Not to cover up your own inability to understand the source text, but for example to explain that a legal concept that exists in the source language may not exist in the target language. A typical example is the proper name of a legal enactment. Where there is no official translation, I would suggest that you write out the proper name and then provide an explanatory translation in brackets.

Naturally the amount of time taken in checking and verification is far greater than for a text intended for information only. Incidentally, patent translations should be included in this category.

Notarisation or certification?

Translations for notarisation or certification demand the same level of quality control as for legal translations. The difference between the two is that you sign your name to confirm the quality of the translation you have produced. Since the legal system in England is based on common law, there are no sworn translators. Consequently, each single translation needs to be sworn instead.

Until a few years ago, it was necessary to take any translation requiring legal credibility to a Notary Public. This meant travelling to the office of the Notary and signing a statement in front of him which he then witnessed and affixed his stamp (and charged you for the service). He did not certify the translation but merely witnessed your signature. There is a new system being introduced now where senior and experienced translators who are full members of the Institute of Translation and Interpreting can certify a translation and affix a seal of authenticity. More details on this are given in Chapter 10.

Incidentally, my philosophy when producing translations for legal purposes, notarisation or certification, is to imagine that I am sitting a translation examination and that my future career depends on the quality of the translation.

7.5   Production capacity

The time allowed to produce a translation is, in my experience, seldom enough. And I must make a confession, I always feel reluctant to part with a translation – just in case I could improve it a little bit more. Such sentiment must however be tempered by commercial realism.

Clients seldom have any idea how long it takes to produce a proper translation. Quite often they will revise the urgency of the work if they realise that you will charge extra if you need to work overtime. We as translators must have the long-term goal of getting clients to realise that producing good, accurate translations takes time. Similarly, clients must be aware that the level of quality control that is possible in a short time is limited.

I think it would be worth looking at a few statistics in this context. Since I ran a translation company for 15 years, I have a good idea what the company's production statistics looked like. Staff translators produce on average around 35,000 words a month. This workload includes checking the equivalent number of words produced by other translators. This works out at about 1,500 words a day.

I know that I am capable of keying in 9,000 words in a day, but that is an unrealistic figure to work on since it cannot be sustained and does not include any quality control. It also means that I work a much longer day – tiredness creeps in and this inevitably leads to mistakes.

If you can dictate your translations, you can achieve a higher work rate. Again, from experience, I know that I can dictate in the region of 2,200 words an hour. The mental effort required for this is far greater than when I actually key the work in directly. Naturally enough, it is not possible to sustain this mental effort all day long. The amount of checking you need to do is also far greater since it is impractical in some cases to go back and re-dictate a section of text if you want to make changes. Not only that, mishearing/misspelling on the part of the typist may alter the meaning of the text.

The time taken to check someone else's translation depends on the quality of the translation, the quality of the source text, and the degree of checking required. A text can be quickly scanned to ensure that everything has been translated and that figures/dates are correct but, as the name suggests, this is only a simple check carried out quickly. Proper word-for-word checking takes a lot more time. Assuming that the translation is of a good draft standard, a competent checker is able to check in the region of 1500 words an hour. This equates roughly to about 5 pages of A4.

If a translation is going to be used for publicity or marketing, it will also need to be checked and edited by a competent copywriter or editor. Likewise it may need localisation. Consequently, if time or resources are not available to do these tasks, then the quality of the finished article will suffer.

Production capacity using translation tools

As the use of translation tools becomes more widespread there will inevitably be the perception that the computer is doing the work and fees should be in relation to this. The strongest argument that we as translators must make is that the client is paying for the translator's intellectual and professional skills as 'knowledge workers'. The translator may use translation tools to facilitate translation production but the process still needs the translator to make the appropriate intelligent decisions and intellectual choice.

The client benefits by the translator using translation tools, such as translation memories and terminology tools, in a number of ways:

- absolute consistency in the use of terminology
- faster turnaround
- previous translations are available as reference since they are stored in electronic format and are thus easier to retrieve than hard copy.

7.6   Be honest with the client

It is always tempting to accept an assignment even if you are short of time. It is up to us translators to try and educate clients and get them to accept that good, accurate translation takes time. When faced with unrealistic or even impossible deadlines, we decline the work – and explain why. We would rather turn down work than produce a poor quality translation that could damage our reputation.

There are times, of course, when you need to work to an absolute deadline. This is usually the result of poor planning by the client. For example, we have a client who was working on a major project in Sweden. The client had staff working in Stockholm who flew out early on a Monday morning and returned on Friday afternoon. Quite often we received a frantic call for translation work to be done that Friday afternoon so that the English could be studied over the weekend prior to somebody returning to Stockholm on the Monday morning. What we did in such cases was tell the client that the time available did not allow for checking. We also made sure that a running heading on each page stated that the translation was an unchecked draft only. The text was checked at the first opportunity on Monday and the client made aware of any significant changes.

7.7 Problems faced by the individual freelance

I was very fortunate when I worked for a translation company since I could pass my translations to my colleagues for checking. The vast majority of translators work as individual freelances and do not have this option. The problem then arises over who is going to check the translation?

Checking your own work is a very subjective exercise. You see what you want to see. There are the standard checks that you can make (I listed these earlier on). You can of course consult a colleague or a client if you have any queries. Similarly, you could ask a colleague to check your work. However, I know from experience that translators are a strange lot and do not accept criticism of their work very lightly. In fact, I have heard said that 'All translators are prima donnas!'. A bold statement, but not untrue in many cases. If you cannot get a colleague to check your work, then try at least to put it aside for as long as possible before checking it. This will allow you to look at it with fresh eyes. Allow sufficient time for checking – a translation leaves something to be desired if it obviously reads like a translation.

If you work for agencies, it is tempting to think that they will check the work anyway. It is, however, your responsibility to provide the best possible translation you can without expecting the agency to tidy up your translation. The company that I worked for checked work wherever possible but this does not absolve the freelance from his responsibility of providing an accurate and acceptable translation. (The client is always advised if checking is not possible as a consequence of time constraints, for example.) Naturally, if the agency finds out that it needs to do additional work on your translation then, it will use other translators instead who are able to provide better quality. Furthermore, you as the original translator may find yourself being charged for any additional work the agency needed to do to bring your translation up to standard!

7.8 Quality takes time and costs money

What you can charge for a translation depends on the level of quality you produce. Some clients are unaware of the need for independent checking and localisation. This is why it is so important to ask the client what the translation is going to be used for. The following illustrates the phases a translation goes through at a translation company.

It is unreasonable for the client to demand the unrealistic or the impossible. Just imagine the reaction you would get if you went to your local garage with the demand, 'My car needs servicing and I want it back by 3 this afternoon!'. The garage will no doubt be booked up for several days ahead. You will have to take your car when the garage has the time and resources to do the work. Furthermore, you will have to pay the garage's bill before you can get your car back!

Clients must be educated to understand the amount of time it takes to produce a trans-

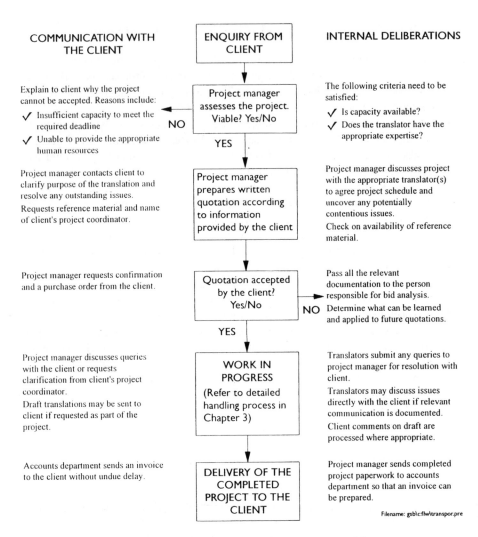

| COMMUNICATION WITH THE CLIENT | ENQUIRY FROM CLIENT | INTERNAL DELIBERATIONS |

Explain to client why the project cannot be accepted. Reasons include:

✓ Insufficient capacity to meet the required deadline

✓ Unable to provide the appropriate human resources

Project manager assesses the project. Viable? Yes/No — **NO**

YES

The following criteria need to be satisfied:

✓ Is capacity available?

✓ Does the translator have the appropriate expertise?

Project manager contacts client to clarify purpose of the translation and resolve any outstanding issues. Requests reference material and name of client's project coordinator.

Project manager prepares written quotation according to information provided by the client

Project manager discusses project with the appropriate translator(s) to agree project schedule and uncover any potentially contentious issues.

Check on availability of reference material.

Project manager requests confirmation and a purchase order from the client.

Quotation accepted by the client? Yes/No — **NO**

YES

Pass all the relevant documentation to the person responsible for bid analysis. Determine what can be learned and applied to future quotations.

Project manager discusses queries with the client or requests clarification from client's project coordinator.

Draft translations may be sent to client if requested as part of the project.

WORK IN PROGRESS
(Refer to detailed handling process in Chapter 3)

Translators submit any queries to project manager for resolution with client.

Translators may discuss issues directly with the client if relevant communication is documented.

Client comments on draft are processed where appropriate.

Accounts department sends an invoice to the client without undue delay.

DELIVERY OF THE COMPLETED PROJECT TO THE CLIENT

Project manager sends completed project paperwork to accounts department so that an invoice can be prepared.

Filename: gsb\c:flw\transpor.pre

Figure 16.   Translation process from enquiry to delivery

lation. It's not just a case of reading the source text and letting the words of the target language flow from our fingers. We may need to do additional research, pick the brains of colleagues, or even spend a significant amount of time formatting the text to suit the client's requirements.

I am not advocating that you antagonise your clients by telling them that they will have to wait a week before you start the translation and that they will have to pay cash on delivery. We as translators do, however, have an obligation to the profession as a whole to make clients aware that translating is a very demanding occupation and that quality does take time and it does cost money. An example of the procedure adopted for quality control that could be used within a translation company or group is shown in the following.

There is always the dilemma that somebody else may be prepared to do the work within the client's deadline. You must make the choice as to whether you accept the work and that you can produce work according to the client's specifications within the required deadline. There is no easy answer to this unless the profession as a whole does some serious client education.

7.9   Pre-emptive measures

There are fundamental questions you must ask before accepting a translation assignment:

- What is the subject? Do I feel confident with my knowledge of this subject?
- Could I see a few typical example pages for assessment?
- What is the volume of work and when is it required by?
- What is the translation going to be used for? Information, publication or legal purposes?
- Are previous translations or reference material available?
- Is anybody available to answer any queries?
- In what form is the translation to be presented?
- Will the client be sending the translation to a foreign subsidiary for checking? If so, can constructive comments be relayed back to me?
- Is there a particular house style to be adhered to?

Determining the quality of a translation is a very difficult exercise and perhaps the commonest cause of dispute. (If everybody were to produce the same style of translation then life would be very boring.) Personal style is all important and my own style may differ to the style adopted by the client. When faced with this problem, and if I am fully confident about the accuracy of my translation, I offer the following statement for the client to consider. 'If I were to give a translation to ten translators, I would not receive ten identical translations. Yet each translation would be equally valid.'

7.10   Quality control operations

Different quality control operations during the translation process should be recorded on an appropriate form. A simple model is shown on page 108.

Form P/1, Issue I

WORK ORDER FORM
TRANSLATIONS

GSB Consulting Ltd
100 Northcott, Bracknell, Berkshire RG12 7WS
- Tel: 01344 319570 ● Fax: 01344 319571
- Mobile: 0771 8900431
- Email: info@gsbconsulting.co.uk

Job Number [　　　　]

Customer order details

Name: [　　　　]

P/O: [　　　] Virus Ch.? [ ] Yes [ ] No

Date/time received: [/ /02] [　　]

Ref. mat? Yes [ ] No [ ] Return? [　]

Invoice information

Invoice total: [£/SEK/Euro]

Exchange rate: [£ = 　 SEK/Euro]

£ equivalent [£　　　]

VAT? [£　　] Inv. total: [£　　]

Posted to client:　　Filed for book-keeping

[/ /02]　　[/ /02]

Assignment details

Language: [ ] [ ] [ ]

Word count: [　　　　] (S/T?) [ ]

Editing/proofing: [ ] Time: [　]

Notes:

Express charge: [ ] 25% [ ] 50% [ ]100%

Certification fee - £25 or equivalent

Quality of source material

Clarity of language: [　　　]

Use of style sheets: [　　　]

Other comments: [　　　]

Delivery instructions and pre-delivery checks

Date due: [/ /02] Time: [　　] S/W format: W4W [ ] Other [　　]

Date sent: [/ /02] Time: [　　] Delivery method: Post? [ ] Fax? [ ] Email? [ ]

General translation checks

- [ ] Compliance with client's requirements
- [ ] Draft translation
- [ ] Check for completeness
- [ ] 1st proof read against source document
- [ ] Spell check
- [ ] Revision against source document
- [ ] Incorporation of changes
- [ ] Final spell check
- [ ] 2nd proof read against source document
- [ ] Final edits and pre-delivery formatting

Checks when using TRADOS

(Additional checks performed when TRADOS software is used to facilitate translation)

- [ ] Close all translation segments and file before cleaning up translation
- [ ] Use TRADOS Tools to clean draft translation
- [ ] Check formatting after cleaning
- [ ] Final edits and pre-delivery formatting
- [ ] Edit .BAK file if necessary

Date/initials on completion of pre-delivery checks and moving completed file to ARCHIVE

[/ /02] [　　]

Filename: C:\fg\Work Order Form P1- I.prz
Revised 15 May 2002

Disposal date [/ /2005]

Figure 17.　Example of a Job Sheet used for recording job details and quality control

Translation

Translation is not a quality control operation per se but its quality sets the tone of the final product. The quality of the translation you produce will however be governed by the quality of the source text. This encroaches on translation theory and is not within the scope of this book.

Glossary compilation

When working with new material it is always helpful to draw up a glossary of unknown terms or terms that are specific to a given client. Whether you do this by reading the text before you start or as you are working through the text depends on your own way of working. I tend to go straight into a text and list unknown items as I am going along. Some of the questions may be answered as you continue with the text. Mark any items clearly in the text so that you can pay particular attention to them when you come to proof reading and editing.

Armed with your list of queries, you can approach your client for an explanation. After all, your client knows his own business (or should do). There are occasions, however, when it is obvious that the author has not read through the text and, when confronted with your query, will alter the text accordingly.

Spell checking

Having a spell checking program is not only necessary but an indispensable tool. A word of caution however: it will indicate only that a word is incorrectly spelt or unrecognisable. It will not tell you that you have used a word that is out of context (tow as opposed to two, for example). Its greatest advantage is clearing up all the small irritating typing mistakes that are so difficult to spot, particularly when checking your own work.

Don't forget to repeat the spell check after having incorporated editorial changes.
As programs become more advanced, additional features such as grammar checking are provided. Microsoft Word for Windows provides a grammar checking facility which also incorporates spell checking. This is in addition to the standard spell checking facility.

Such facilities are a real boon to the translator since they question anything that the program does not recognise. 'Constructive criticism' offered by a computer is entirely impersonal and can be accepted or rejected without the translator's pride being compromised.

Proof reading (own work)

Proof reading your own work is perhaps the most difficult task in the process of translation. And spell checking is definitely not a substitute. Put your translation to one side for as long as possible when you have completed the first draft. To illustrate this point, look at a translation that you did perhaps two years ago and see what changes, if any, you would make.

Try to follow a number of simple rules when proof reading:

- Make sure that you have translated everything by checking page against page, paragraph against paragraph, table contents against table contents. This may seem elementary but being disturbed by the phone, for example, can cause you to restart elsewhere in the text – particularly if sections are similar. Use a ruler to mark your place in the source text as you work through line by line.
- There are occasions where you will split or merge paragraphs, so take this into consideration when checking contents against contents.
- Make sure that the headings in the Contents agree with the headings in the body of the text. Most software packages allow you to compile a Contents List from the text – you'll learn all these features as you become more experienced.
- Consider the items you marked for particular attention.
- Read your text as a piece of original text and not as a translation. Does anything sound strange? Can you recognise the structure and syntax of the source language?
- Check names and numbers.
- Read again as a piece of original text once you have incorporated all your edits.
- Run the spell check once more.

The following appeared on our notice board some while back. No source was quoted so I hope the original writer who penned these lines does not feel his copyright is breached maliciously.

Once upon a time I used
To mispell,
To sometimes split infinitives
To get words of out order
To, punctuate badly
To confused my tenses,
To deem old word wondrous fair,
to ignore capitals,
To employ common or garden clichés,
To miss the occasional out,
To engage in tautological, repetitive statements
To exaggerate hundreds of times a day,
And to repeat puns quite by chants.
But worst of all I used
To forget to finish what

Having to learn a new set of rules is always tiresome. It is all very well to use your own marking symbols but what if somebody else needs to interpret your correction marks. If you use clear, legible standardised symbols then this will facilitate the work of the person incorporating corrections. Standard proof marks are given in British Standard BS 5261: Part 2: 1976. Tables of the most frequent marks that the translator or checker will need are given in the Appendix.

Checking (other person's work)

It is a fact of life that it is far easier to see other people's mistakes than your own. You will be able to walk past somebody else's computer and spot a mistake on screen instantaneously. This is why having the work checked by a second person is invaluable. The operations involved are essentially the same as when proof reading your own work.

Ignore the source text initially and read the target language text as though it were a piece of original writing and not a translation. Refer to the source text only after having read the translation. Then repeat the exercise of making sure that everything has been translated.

One of the most sensitive considerations when checking another person's text is style. Style is so individual and criticism is not accepted lightly. If the translation is correct, and the style is not inappropriate, leave well alone. Any piece of text can be rewritten – just consider how a tabloid newspaper reports the same event compared with a quality newspaper.

Bear in mind the difference between checking and editing. Checking is intended to bring factual errors and inconsistencies to the attention of the original translator. Editing is revising the text for a specific purpose and goes beyond what the translator is normally asked to do.

Checking and proof reading take time if they are to be done properly. It takes about an hour to proof read about 5 pages of translated text and compare it with the original (assuming about 300 words per page).

A text can also be scan checked. This merely determines whether or not all the text has been fully translated but includes spot checks to determine the quality of the actual translation. These may indicate whether complete checking of the actual translation is warranted.

Updating own work with checker's/quality controller's or client's revisions of draft

This is self-explanatory. You may wish to disregard some of the comments, particularly if they concern individual style and not syntax or technical errors. You'll need to be diplomatic about client's comments – if they are obviously incorrect then the fact will need to be noted.

Desk top publishing

Desk top publishing is not essentially quality control but quality of presentation. There is the advantage, of course, that an additional pair of eyes will read through the text.

Incorporation of client's revisions of final copy

There is a standing joke that you will not see the last mistake in a text until it has been printed and ready for distribution. Where does the responsibility lie? It is often difficult to assess the appearance of a document until it is in its printed state.

Producing a copy using DTP allows you and the client to see what the document will look like when it is printed. This is when the client may wish to make aesthetic changes that may make demands on your editing skills – shortening the text to fill a given space, for example. Many clients are unaware that a translation may not necessarily generate the same volume of text as the source language.

Final spell check

It's worth running a final spell check after implementing all the editorial changes to your translated text. In fact, it's no more than common sense.

7.11   Deadlines

It is unfortunate that, in many cases, it is the client who dictates or attempts to impose a deadline. It is up to the translation profession to endeavour to educate clients by stating that adequate time is necessary to do a good job. Of course, this attitude must be tempered by commercial considerations. If you can't do the job in time then there is somebody else willing to sacrifice leisure time to meet the client's demands.

I have seen many examples where a client has spent a long time plus considerable resources on producing a complex bid for a particular project and has then approached the translator with the demand that a translation be completed by a given time. The client is of course working to a fixed deadline for submitting his bid but has given little consideration to the fact that the translator needs adequate time to do his part of the work. This is, of course, a prime case for making an additional charge for working unsociable hours.

7.12   Splitting a translation between several translators

As I have said already, a translation should ideally be done by one person. This avoids conflicts over style, choice of terminology, formatting and other considerations. Some problems can be avoided by having a project coordinator who is responsible for the final document. But this is not always a practical consideration among freelances unless a specific fee is agreed for coordination and harmonisation.

Each of the translators involved needs to be furnished with the following information at the start of the project:

- The name and telephone number of the project coordinator.
- A project schedule showing the planned progress of the work.
- Who is responsible for translating and checking the different sections:
  - Specific layout requirements:
  - left, right, top and bottom margins,
  - typeface or style sheet,
  - pagination.
- Glossary of terms to be used.
- Reference material.

Since there is always disparity in style and choice of terminology, it is advisable in members of the group work to produce a glossary as the project progresses. Again, one person should accept responsibility for keeping this updated. The use of computer-aided translation and terminology management software can facilitate this.

Most freelances live a fairly isolated existence and may find it hard to work together with others on a project. Working on a common project can be very rewarding since those involved can learn from other members of the team.

7.13 Translation reports

There are occasions when it is impossible to resolve queries that arise during the course of translation. This usually happens if the author of the text is not available or has not replied to your queries before the translation is due for delivery. It is then worth listing your queries and any presumptions you may have made or any action taken.

The intention should be for a translation report to contain constructive comments. There will be many occasions when a source text contains spelling errors, ambiguities and omissions. It is surprising how many documents have not been checked before being submitted for translation.

It is also useful for a translation checker to submit a report if the translation has been done by a freelance translator. Ignorance is bliss and, unless constructive comments are made known to the translator, there is no opportunity for improvement. One of the disadvantages of being a freelance translator and working in isolation is the lack of feedback and, unless this is provided, all is considered right with the world.

8 Presentation and delivery of translations

> '*A neat rivulet of text shall meander through a meadow of margin.*'
> Richard Sheridan, 1751–1816

The level of presentation that can be achieved on a personal computer is very advanced. In the space of 25 or so years the level of technology available, and affordable, has gone from a correctable golfball typewriter (costing around £600 in 1977) to a basic personal computer with an inexpensive printer for about the same price. If you consider what this means in real terms then the pace of technological change and the fall in prices for sophisticated equipment is quite amazing.

Computers are excellent if not indispensable tools and, if you take the time and trouble to do the tutorial provided with your software package, they can perform wonders. It is of course very tempting to go straight ahead and use the software since most programs are very easy to use and have help available at the touch of a key. There are certain fundamentals worth considering that will facilitate any subsequent work.

8.1 Thou shalt not use the spacebar!

If you are providing your work on disk to a client, there will probably be work done subsequently on the layout. The resulting layout will differ considerably according to the font and size of character you use. The choice will be determined by the printer you have. A basic dot matrix printer may offer but a single typeface – usually Courier 10, whereas a laser printer may offer at least 35 fonts in sizes from around 4 points up to 150 points. (Courier 10 corresponds to around 12 points – 1 point = 1/72″).

The sizes on the next page indicate part of the range available on a postscript printer compared with Courier 10. This book, for example, was produced and typeset in Times Roman 10 points (for the most part) using Word for Windows software and a Hewlett Packard 2000C inkjet printer.

Courier 10

PEPITA 10 POINTS

Helvetica Oblique 10 points

Gill Sans 14 points

ALGERIAN 20 POINTS ... *and so on.*

For these reasons **you should not use the spacebar to format the position of text**. This will work of course but, if any subsequent editing needs to be done, all the spaces will need to be removed.

This advice may sound quite elementary but it is a nightmare for anyone who has to remove the spaces and properly align the work using the indent or tab keys. Likewise you should set the minimum number of tabs for each application rather than using the defaults provided by the program you are using.

It is of course convenient to use the default tab settings, which are usually every 0.5', but they are somewhat restrictive. Using the centred, right and decimal tabs can save a lot of time once you become familiar with their use. The following is an example of text formatted using Courier 10 font and the spacebar:

Fruit	Colour	Weight	Price
Apples	Red	100 g	25p
Oranges	Orange	150 g	30p
Peaches	Peach	75 g	30p
Chinese gooseberries	Green	30 g	25p

The text is neatly aligned since it was written using a fixed space font where all characters and spaces have the same width. When the text is given a different font, its appearance changes dramatically even though nothing has been changed in the text. All the work of putting in spaces has to be undone and tabs inserted so that the text can be worked on. The following happens if the font is changed (even though the layout may appear to be the same on screen):

Fruit	Colour	Weight	Price
Apples	Red	100 g	25p
Oranges	Orange	150 g	30p
Peaches	Peach	75 g	30p
Chinese gooseberries	Green	30 g	25p

Desk top publishing has become a reality and the facilities available in a standard word processing package such as Microsoft Word running on a PC or a Macintosh are quite amazing. You will usually be provided with specific layout instructions where these are required. The job of the translator is not just being a wordsmith!

I suppose there is the argument that your client is paying for a translation and not aesthetically-pleasing presentation. Similarly, a poor translation is not going to be enhanced just because it is beautifully presented. However, if you take a lot of care in the presentation of your work, the argument is that you are likely to be just as quality-conscious about the actual translation. Consider the following two paragraphs and table. The texts are identical but the layout has been enhanced with very little effort.

Text written with a typeface such as Courier 10 is fairly bland and monotonous. It was designed to be used on typewriters where each character occupied exactly the same space on a line. It provided very little variation apart from underlining. Features such as emboldening were not readily available. By using different fonts and proportional spacing, the presentation of a document can be considerably enhanced. Likewise, the presentation of tables can be improved by the table features in word processing programs.

Simple table	Heading 1	Heading 2	Heading 3
Item 1	123	456	789
Item 2	789	123	456
Total	912	579	1245

Text written with a typeface such as Courier 10 is fairly bland and monotonous. It was designed to be used on typewriters where each character occupied exactly the same space on a line. It provided very little variation apart from underlining.

Features such as **emboldening** were not readily available. *By using different fonts and proportional spacing, the presentation of a document can be considerably enhanced.* Likewise, the presentation of tables can be improved by the table features in word processing programs.

Table functions are an easy way of setting up tabs since the table format is 'elastic' and can be changed without having to reset fixed tab positions.

You can instruct the program not to display the table lines once you have entered all the necessary data. See what your program has to offer and choose the method that suits you best.

Simple table	Heading 1	Heading 2	Heading 3
Item 1	123	456	789
Item 2	789	123	456
Total	912	579	1245

8.2 Setting up columns

The range of facilities offered by word processing programs is considerable.

The level of presentation that is possible will be determined by the degree of sophistication provided by the printer you have at your disposal.

Setting up columns, as in this case is a simple task and fairly straightforward.

Columns can be used to match the layout of the translation to the original but do take additional time.

Of course, the presentation may be dictated by the client but you must charge accordingly.

You may wish to present your translations as 'perfect' reproductions of the original interns of content and layout. This can be used as a selling point but, again, takes time.

It is also worth considering that there will be disparity between the number of source language and target language words. This, in turn will affect layout and you may not be able to squeeze all the translation into the space available.

The client may not be aware of this phenomenon so it may well be worth mentioning the fact.

The difference may be as much as 30% in some cases. See the example below.

Cutting down the length of text after translation can be a messy job.

8.3 Text expansion

Consider the text *'Crème traitante enrichie au sérum naturel'*. Compare this with its translations into English, German, Spanish and Italian.

Crème traitante enrichie au sérum naturel
Hand treatment cream enriched with natural serum
Handpflegecreme, angereichert mit natürlichem Serum
Crema tratante para las manos enriquecida con suero natural
Crema per il trattamento delle mani arricchita con siero naturale

8.4 Macros

Most programs have excellent tutorials and the time spent learning some of the useful features will be time well spent. I know from experience that time is inevitably in short supply when you are doing an assignment but I have always tried to set aside say half an hour at the end of the working day, when using a new software package, to look at a feature that can rationalise my work. (If all else fails – read the instructions!)

The use of macros or a built-in glossary feature saves a lot of time. Consider a text where you may need to write long, official names such as *The County Administrative Court* in a legal translation. Rather than write this out in full each time, you can construct a macro which you call up each time with a few keystrokes.

It's worth setting up macros for repeat items. Depending on the program you use, you can set up macros for a range of operations. This is but one of the many tools available to facilitate and enhance presentation. Read the manual and see how this can help your work.

8.5 Desk top publishing

The level of technology required for producing standard translations need not be highly sophisticated. Programs such as Microsoft Word provide a broad spectrum of facilities, most of which will never be used by the translator. There are occasions however where the client has a manual on disk and will have invested considerable resources in its production. You may be called upon to 'overtype' the original to save the task of having to re-do layouts, tables, graphics and other enhancements.

It is on such occasions that DTP facilities are required. You should have gained a reasonable level of experience and confidence with your computer before attempting such work. DTP programs are not designed for word processing but text processing, page layouts, being able to import graphics and other files from various software packages. To operate efficiently they need a fairly powerful PC, a good-sized monitor (at least 20″) and an appropriate printer. Consequently they are perhaps beyond the scope of the inexperienced.

8.6 Compatibility between different PC packages

The ways in which various presentation features are devised in different programs are not the same. If you use a different program to the client, and the client is going to do additional text processing on your electronic file, there is seldom any point in spending time on including presentation features such as emboldening or italics. Why? The program to which your text file is to be exported will probably not recognise the software commands for these features and they will not appear when the client brings your file up on screen.

Only experience will show how 'compatible' different packages are. Likewise, there are different ways of saving a file so that it can be used in another software program. If, for example in WordPerfect, you save your work as a 'generic file', it will strip out all the extraneous formatting features. It will also take out all characters with diacritics such as â, å or ø. As a consequence, all these characters will be gone when you import the file into a different package.

This is becoming less of an issue because of better compatibility but problems still arise.

Printouts produced on printers made by the same manufacturers, for example a Hewlett Packard 1600C InkJet and a Hewlett Packard LaserJet 4M Plus, will differ. So beware!

8.7 Electronic publishing

While revising this book, I have tried to give a glimpse of developing technologies and practices that the translator may need to consider in the not too distant future. Hence this reference to electronic publishing.

The number of documents that are now produced in non-electronic form is getting ever smaller. Although the level of compatibility between various software programs is fairly sophisticated, each program uses its own way of marking-up or 'tagging' documents. Just look at the way Word for Windows and WordPerfect for Windows mark up text using style sheets, for example. The codes used for this are usually hidden but can be revealed in some cases.

It is beyond the scope of this book to look at all the different systems in use but systems are emerging which will be in widespread use in the very near future. The following page shows an example of specific markup typically found in word processing systems in the form of invisible codes that instruct the program to perform functions associated with formatting. It shows raw text in its unformatted state, specific markup, and the text in its formatted state.

In addition to specific markup systems there are general systems. The two most common are **SGML** (Standard Generalised Markup Language) and **ODA** (Office Document Architecture). These formal standards are open and not under the control of one company or country. While PostScript is the *de facto* standard page description language, the structure and infinite variations in a document can be precisely described by SGML. ODA is similar to SGML in that it describes a document as a hierarchical set of objects. The terminology that ODA uses is different to that used by SGML.

Other formats such as HTML are coming to the fore. Similarly, the translation of Web pages is becoming a market for the translator, albeit a specialised one. While the translator will eventually be faced with dealing with these, they are perhaps beyond the scope of this book. If you plan to use translation memory systems, the software will have the functionality to deal with HTML.

> The Constitution of the United States of America PREAMBLE We the people of the United States, in order to form a more perfect Union, establish justice, insure domestic tranquility, provide for the common defense, promote the general welfare, and secure the blessings of liberty to ourselves and our posterity, do ordain and establish this Constitution for the United States of America.

`[Fontsize+2]` `[BoldItalics][centre]The` `Constitution of the[hardReturn]` `United States of America` `[fontNormal][fontsize2]` `PREAMBLE[leftjustify][all caps]` We the people `[notall caps]` of the United States, in order to form a more perfect `[italics]` Union, `[fontNormal]` establish justice, insure domestic tranquility, provide for the common defense, promote the general welfare, and secure the blessings of liberty to ourselves and our posterity, do ordain and establish this Constitution for the United States of America.	***The Constitution of the United States of America*** PREAMBLE WE THE PEOPLE of the United States, in order to form a more perfect *Union*, establish justice, insure domestic tranquility, provide for the common defense, promote the general welfare, and secure the blessings of liberty to ourselves and our posterity, do ordain and establish this Constitution for the United States of America.

Figure 17. Example of SGML mark-up

8.8 Getting the translation to the client

There are several ways of getting work to your client depending on urgency. Before you agree to send any work to a client by a method that incurs additional costs, make sure you agree with the client who should pay. If the urgency is demanded by the client then the client should pay. The options available are: post, fax, electronic mail and couriers. You can of course deliver the translation yourself but this is seldom practical and your time is too valuable to act as an unpaid courier.

Most of the options considered in the first edition of this book have now been superseded by the use of electronic mail but are still worth mentioning since original documents such as certified translations and original will need to be sent by post or courier.

Postal service

For the most part, the Post Office provides an acceptable service with a large percentage of first class deliveries reaching their destination the next day. There are times however when deliveries are less than reliable, particularly if there is unforeseen industrial action.

Even using 'Special Delivery' and paying a hefty surcharge provides no guarantee whatsoever of delivery the next day, although the service is more secure than First Class. The only consolation is that you will get the surcharge refunded. This is however of no use whatsoever if the translation has not arrived on time. 'Datapost' is supposedly guaranteed but is very expensive by comparison. Again make sure that the client agrees to accept these additional costs if the service is demanded. These services change so check with your post office for the latest information.

Dependence on the postal system is becoming less of an issue since most work is received and delivered electronically. The only time I use the post office is to send original documents and certified translations to the client.

Fax

The fax (or facsimile transmission machine) is a wonderful piece of equipment. It is excellent for getting information backwards and forwards almost instantaneously. The quality of the copy provided is not, however, as good as an original. There are still applications where a dedicated fax is useful.

Electronic mail

This facility is now being used by most translators. There are still some teething troubles, most of which are caused by slight differences in equipment specifications. For the most part the equipment operates without problems. The additional equipment you will need is a modem but this is now incorporated in most new computers. It is preferable to have an additional telephone line for your voice phone and data transfer service.

As the computer capacity required to operate ever-increasingly sophisticated software packages becomes greater, the amount of information you need to send down the telephone line grows at the same rate.

Some modem transmission protocols have built-in compression and decompression features to cut down on transmission times. There are also separate packages available which compress the text before you go into the actual data transmission. This is an important consideration when sending files to a different country since this allows you to keep telephone charges lower.

Fax facilities used by translators operate at a speed of 14,400 baud (bits/s). The first modem I used some fifteen years ago struggled to run at 300 baud! Higher speeds are available but both the transmitting modem and the receiving modem must be able to run at the faster speed. Much higher speeds are available for standard telephone lines but the quality of the transmission line can restrict the speed. Quoting transmission speeds is folly since present speeds will seem painfully slow in a very short space of time.

ISDN (Integrated Services Digital Network) is a system now available to greatly increase the capacity of telephone networks. It will offer features such as caller identification, fast fax, and clearer and faster transmission. Other developments will no doubt make even this facility seem archaic.

Broadband technology that allows much higher transmission speeds is becoming more widely available but there are limitations imposed by the proximity to the broadband station. In general you need to be nearer than 5 km from the station but be aware that this is not the geographical, straightline distance but the distance the supply cable covers to reach you.

There are several organisations that provide electronic mailbox or bulletin board systems. These services allow you to rent an electronic mailbox where you can store or pick up electronic mail. They also give you access to a range of web sites and other sources of information. Observe a suitable level of security when communicating with the outside world via electronic means. This is particularly important if you leave your computer in host mode and unattended. This is not unusual if you have a client in a different time zone and he sends files to you outside your normal office hours.

Never, but never, open files where they is no sender indicated or where you do not recognise the sender. If you open an attachment from an unknown sender that ends in .exe you are asking for trouble. If you are in any doubt do not open the email but send a reply stating that you policy is not to open files from unknown sources and requesting that the sender identifies himself then delete the email.

Road and air couriers

There was a time, before the advent of electronic mail, when we used international couriers all the time to get urgent documents delivered abroad. We use the service less frequently now but it is still very useful if original documents need to be delivered quickly. Again, make sure you agree with the client who is going to pay.

Local couriers are sometimes necessary, particularly when dealing with documents that cannot be sent by electronic mail. As in the case of all outside services, make sure that you use a reputable company even though it may cost a little more.

I can quote an example to illustrate this from when I managed a translation company. We had agreed to send an assignment to be translated by a freelance by a given deadline for a new client. One of the client's executives had booked a ticket on a plane to go to an important meeting in Paris with a contract proposal. The translator had agreed to do the work in good time for it to be checked and printed on the client's headed paper by us before delivery.

The translator was late in finishing the work so we organised a courier to pick up the translation. The courier set off late, got stuck in traffic and then got a puncture on the way to the translator. The courier found that his spare tyre was also flat. Rather than phone for a backup, the courier left the vehicle and walked, yes walked, to the nearest garage to get the puncture mended! By this time the client was getting frantic and the translator became understandably neurotic. We were the 'piggy in the middle'.

The outcome was that the client missed the flight to Paris and had to postpone the meeting. It turned out that the client was somebody I had worked for before and with whom I had established a track record. The company had changed its name in the meantime but still had my name on its records.

Had this been a genuinely new client, it would probably have been the first and last job we would have done for them.

9 What to do if things go wrong

'Experience, the name men give to their mistakes.'
Oscar Wilde, 1854–1900

This is not a doomsday philosophy – it's being realistic. Occasionally things will go wrong. Accepting that this can be the case heightens your awareness of the fact and, subconsciously, you implement the necessary measures to prevent, or at least limit, the effects of factors that may be within your power to resolve. To err is human and to do so is often the only way to learn so make sure the opportunity is not wasted.

It is most unfortunate if things go wrong the first time you do work for a client. You will not have established a track record and may not get a second chance. So do your level best to make sure things go right every time. Above all, avoid getting into a situation where you have to say,

> **Oh, I'm sorry, there must have been some misunderstanding**

9.1 Preventive measures

Probably the greatest cause of aggravation is missing a deadline. There is only one course of action you can take if this happens – grasp the nettle, ring the client, and explain honestly what has happened. If you ring ahead of the deadline when you are aware that a delay might be inevitable, your explanation may be more readily accepted. Don't for goodness' sake exceed the deadline and remain silent hoping that the client may not notice. It is essential to keep the client aware of any schedule disruption.

I know it sounds bureaucratic but put everything in writing. This is all part of accountability and is the essence of quality assurance. I have seen so many examples where a delivery date has been agreed on the promise of a client providing you with the work on a given date. Even though the client is late, he will still expect you to deliver on time despite the change in circumstances. Email or send a fax to the client stating that you received the job later than promised and are therefore concerned that you will not be able to keep to the agreed delivery date.

It's worth considering what might cause a delay – this will at least allow you to be prepared with the necessary contingency measures:

- The job has not arrived, as agreed, from the client. If there has been a delay in the post, keep the envelope and make a note of the time and date when it arrived. This won't make any difference to the particular job you are working on but, if you send it to your local Post Office sorting office demanding an explanation, it might improve services later on. The level of service provided by the Post Office has improved but, unless awareness is drawn to any hitch in the system, there is no chance of any further improvement.
- The job is taking longer than you had anticipated. This is an understandable cause of delay, particularly if you have agreed a deadline without sight of the work. Again, offer a reasonable explanation as to why you consider there could be a delay.
- You are not really happy with the content of the text you are asked to translate. This is an unenviable state of affairs. A good case for not accepting work without sight of the text to be translated.
- You were not able to open an email attachment in the software at your disposal. I have experience trying unsuccessfully to open an attachment and have asked the client to save and re-send the text as an .RTF file which could then be opened

Only genuine explanations for any delay are acceptable. Excuses are usually transparent and will not enhance your reputation. Circumstances beyond your control need to be documented. There have been times in the past when the postal services have been abysmal but now that electronic mail and fax are readily available, you no longer need to be dependent on the vagaries of outside parties.

There may be occasions when your computer is down but these are very rare. Good housekeeping with your disks and backups will lessen the impact of any equipment failure. Likewise, a good service contract will reduce downtime for repairs or service.

Be aware of the risk of computer viruses. If you use original software only and new blank disks that you have formatted yourself then there is little risk that you will encounter these nasties. However as soon as you start communicating with the outside world, either by electronic mail or through the interchange of disks, you become vulnerable.

There are several anti-virus programs now available. They will detect and counteract known viruses thereby providing a level of protection. Whichever protective program you decide to buy, it should be upgraded regularly since new viruses are being invented all the time. Some may be considered 'harmless fun' while others can be completely devastating. What would be your reaction if all the characters on your screen suddenly fell into a heap at the bottom of your screen, or if a file started to multiply itself by copying so that it eventually filled your hard disk?

9.2   Equipment insurance

Whether or not you have equipment insurance depends on circumstances. If you work from home then you may feel reasonably secure. Consider what would happen if you had burglars or a casual vandal gained access to your computer. A computer is easily removed, its useful components stripped out, and the rest disposed of.

Insurance is well advised. It's not so much the loss of the equipment itself but the time and effort spent on the work stored on disk. Software can be replaced or re-installed but the hours you have spent on translation files that are on the hard disk represent a lot of hard work.

The computer may represent a considerable investment. But what of all the hours you have devoted to entering information on the hard disk? All the glossaries you have compiled? It is a very well-disciplined translator who has religiously taken copies of all the information and translations accrued over the years. And hands up all those who store backup disks at a separate location!

If you do have portable equipment or you're transporting your computer in your car, the peace of mind afforded by a special computer policy is well worth the comparatively small outlay.

9.3   Maintenance

A maintenance contract for your computer hardware is rather like insurance. You don't need it until something goes wrong. Major manufacturers of computer hardware often give you the option of a three-year, on-site warrantee for a reasonable charge. I have found this the most suitable arrangement.

When you purchase a piece of equipment, try to get the best deal you can. Most reputable companies offer some form of warranty and, again, you get what you pay for. There are usually two options – return to base, or maintenance on site. You can look at the computer magazines for the best prices for equipment but the lower the price for a given piece of equipment, the lower the value of the warranty.

A lot of standard equipment can be purchased from what are virtually 'cash and carry' stores. Their sales margin is very low and, as a consequence, they are hardly likely to provide a generous warranty. It's as well to be realistic and ask for written details of what any warranty provides. The following points are worth considering:

- What response time is offered?
- Does the agreement covers maintenance on-site?

- Is a replacement machine offered if your machine needs to be returned for repair?
- Are any of the hardware components excluded? Keyboards sometimes are – this is worth considering if you are prone to spilling cups of tea!
- Is maintenance provided by the company offering the service or through a third party contractor? Do you want to pay additional commission to the dealer?

Pre-sales promises are sometimes followed by after-sales disappointments. Find out whether you can pay your maintenance by a monthly standing order through the bank. This way you will have some control over payment if the service provided doesn't come up to scratch or if the company providing the service ceases to operate. Beware also of contracts that are automatically renewed unless cancelled in writing in advance. Three months' notice is sometimes required. The legality of such statements may sometimes be doubtful but you can spend a lot of time and run up unnecessary solicitors' bills resolving the matter, even if you are in the right. Shop around for the best deal but read the small print.

Software maintenance is a different kettle of fish. If you find that your software is corrupt, the supplier will usually replace it for a small charge if you return your original system disk. Providing you have a legal registered copy, you will in many cases receive updates for a nominal charge. Remember – you don't own the software. You have merely purchased a licence to use it subject to given conditions.

9.4   Indemnity insurance

There are translators who consider that indemnity insurance is something they do not need. Although indemnity insurance is not a legal requirement it is worth considering what your position would be if a claim were to be made against you. If you operate as a sole proprietor, your personal possessions and even your home could be sold to pay costs if a successful judgment were made against you.

The value of your invoice for a particular translation may not be very high. Consider the cost incurred by your client if your translation is used in a leaflet which is then printed in colour at a cost that may run into thousands of pounds. If you made a mistake in your translation which is not detected until the leaflet has been mailed to thousands of people . . .

The Institute of Translation and Interpreting administers a scheme for its members. Translators who are not members are advised to contact a reputable professional indemnity insurance broker.

9.5   Clients who are slow payers or who become insolvent

Before you accept any work from a potential client make quite sure that you are happy with the terms of business that are offered. Make sure these terms are in writing and are a bilateral agreement that is implemented. If you don't like the terms then say so and decline the work offered or negotiate terms that you find acceptable.

It is unfortunate that you usually find out the worst when presented with a *fait accompli*. Look for any signs of unnecessarily slow payment or implausible excuses for non-payment. The chances of getting paid once a client has become insolvent are very slim. Make sure that a client does not run up a large bill where non-payment could cause you financial embarrassment.

I would like to quote an example. We had worked for a particular client for some time and, although payment was slow, we eventually got our invoices paid. Our client, in turn, worked for a third party. The third party fell out with our client for reasons beyond our control with the result that our client did not pay his invoices despite endless promises to do so. We eventually took out a county court judgment against our client and the judgment was found in our favour. The client was given a period in which to settle the account but this did not happen and the client pleaded that he had no assets. The case went back to the court and we were obliged to attend a court hearing in the county where the client resided. It took us a couple of hours in atrocious conditions to get to the court. We waited until the appointed time and were called into the courtroom. Our client simply did not turn up. Again he was given time to pay but nothing happened since he had, at least on paper, no assets that a court bailiff could seize.

You as a service provider will probably have no inkling that a client plans to default on payment even though the client may have been aware for some time that he or she is in financial difficulties. Never allow debt to increase to more than you can afford to lose!

When you are starting up in business you are almost obliged to accept the work you are offered. If possible, try to avoid relying too much on any one client. The usual criterion is to make sure that no more than 25% of your income is received from any one source. Consider what could happen if that client decided to change translators or no longer needed your services for any reason.

There are fewer things more disheartening that having to wait an excessive amount of time to get paid for your labours, or not knowing when you might expect payment. So what can you do? If you know your client very well, you could try a light-hearted approach to quicken the conscience. I once sent the following to a client and received a cheque within days.

My bank balance is getting quite fraught
In fact, it's almost down to nought
A cheque would be smashing
It would stop my teeth gnashing
And pay for some things I've just bought

Most agencies pay regularly since there is mutual dependency between freelancers and agencies. Their usual terms are to pay at the end of the month following the month during which you submitted your invoice. If there are specific terms of payment, you do at least know when to expect a cheque and can plan accordingly. The end of the month is however very elastic in some cases and it is these few cases that cause unnecessary difficulty. If you are unsure, you could ask the ITI who are able to advise if any particular agency is tardy. Make sure you agree terms of payment in writing, in advance, before accepting any assignment.

Working for a direct client is more difficult unless you establish from the outset that payment is required by a given date. Ask the client for references if you are in any doubt. Check with the references and do not accept them merely at face value. Be realistic – this is your livelihood! If the client has nothing to hide then offence will not be taken. You will also be considered a serious person to deal with.

Always ask for a written purchase order since it is only in exceptional cases that a client will actually collect and pay for a translation at the same time. Agree on payment in stages, or part payment in advance, if the job takes more than three weeks.

It is unfortunate that a lot of companies attempt to dictate their own terms of payment so it is best to sort out these terms from the outset. It's no use stating terms of payment '30 days net' on your invoice if this is a unilateral declaration. There needs to be mutually-agreed terms.

Set a credit limit. After all, new clients are unknown quantities and you have no way of measuring their reliability or honesty. It will not help matters if a client owes you thousands of pounds for work you have accepted and is then unable to pay. How much can you afford to lose or give away? Would you expect to be offered unlimited credit with no interest charges when out shopping?

If you are asked to submit a written quotation for a large assignment, make sure that you agree terms of payment and other conditions in writing. Verbal agreements are almost valueless, particularly if the person with whom you have made the agreement has left the company by the time you try to get payment.

If you have employed all the usual measures to get paid and are just fobbed off with one excuse after another, waste no further time but take out a county court judgment against the debtor. If the debtor had been a reasonable person and solvent, some attempt would have been made to settle your bill. You can make a small claim, up to £5000, through a county court and you do not need a solicitor for this. The address and telephone number of all county courts are listed in the telephone directory under Courts. Leaflets on alternative dispute resolution are available from your local court to advise you. In some cases the mere threat of legal action through a county court will prompt payment to be made since any judgment against the debtor will have an effect on the debtor's credit rating. If the debtor has gone into receivership, you as a creditor should be informed. The only sound advice is to exercise good debtor control – the longer a bill is left unpaid, the less likely it is to be paid.

Legislation to enforce payment terms and the imposition of penalty interest is now in force. This is called The Late Payment of Commercial Debts (Interest) Act 1998. A guide to this and better payment practice are available on www.payontime.co.uk.

9.6   Excuses offered for late payment

The majority of clients are quite good about payments. However, a few baddies make life difficult at times – usually when the bank manager is breathing down your neck. All manner of excuses will be offered when you try to chase payment. Some explanations are genuine and plausible whereas others are mere procrastination. This makes forecasting cashflow very difficult. You can try applying the following when working out when you might expect payment.

The Law of Delayed Payment:

$$\frac{x+t+h}{s} = P \ (days)$$

where,

$x =$ the terms of payment stated on your invoice, e.g. 30 days. (This is often interpreted by the client as the number of days he can procrastinate before he even bothers to look at the invoice.)

$t =$ is a factor which depends on the excuse applied by the client at the time and is estimated on the basis of the excuses listed below.

$h =$ additional delay resulting from public holidays.

$s =$ $1/n$, where n is the number of people who need to approve payment or sign a cheque.

Excuses for not having paid an invoice are multitude. The following are some of the more common that we have been offered:

1. 'A cheque is in the mail. We posted it yesterday, so you should have received it by now'.
2. 'Oh! Your invoice arrived on my desk just after the last computer run so it won't go in until next month now'.
3. 'The person who deals with invoices/signs the cheques is on holiday/sick/not in at the moment'.
4. 'We don't make payments until we receive a statement'. (Why bother to send an invoice by itself – send an invoice and a statement!)
5. 'I've signed it and passed it on, it's lying on my boss's desk'.
6. 'I've passed it onto accounts'. You phone accounts, 'We haven't received it from the department who ordered the work'. Can anybody define this void that seems to exist between departments and which seems to swallow everything that is in the least bit financially embarrassing?

7. 'We don't seem to have received your invoice yet, perhaps it has got lost in the post. If you send us another copy I'll see that you get paid straight away', . . . and the whole carousel starts again . . .

8. 'Oh, Mr Slydoutovit is no longer with the company, can I help?'.

9. 'Our accounts department is in another building. If I give you the number, you can ring direct. No, I'm sorry, I can't transfer you on this number'.

10. 'Sorry, I can't say – it's in the computer and I can't get at it'.

11. 'Oh, the person that dealt with this died over the holidays and we can't open his desk. Your invoice must be in that lot somewhere'. (X-ray eyes?)

12. 'Our accounts department is in another building and all internal mail goes via the post office. It must have got lost or delayed.'

13. 'Haven't you received our purchase order yet? You need to quote the purchase order number on your invoice before we can approve payment'.

14. 'Our books are with the auditors and we can't issue any cheques at the moment.'

15. 'Our cheque book is locked in the accountant's desk and we have lost the keys.'

These are all excuses we've heard – there are others as you may have experienced. Some are more or less plausible but equally delaying.

The following is worth repetition. ***Prevention is definitely better than cure***. Unless you know a client and his reliability, always ask for a written order, the name of the person placing the order and agree on terms of payment IN WRITING. Agreement over the phone may sound quite satisfactory at the time but becomes very flimsy when trying to extract payment for your labours.

If a job is likely to span more than a few weeks, agree on terms of part payment as the work progresses. This is particularly important if you exclude all other clients while working on one particular task.

I know from personal experience the frustration of trying to get paid by a client who is obviously procrastinating. The only advice I would offer is to be polite, persistent and factual in your approach. Make notes of what has been said or agreed. If it is obvious that the client is being unprofessional, it is helpful if the ITI is informed so that others can be made aware of the problem. If you are dealing with a client in a different country, inform the corresponding translator organisation in that country. Shared intelligence can but benefit other colleagues.

9.7 Checklist for getting paid on time

- Always carry out a credit check on a potential client. Winning a new client is always exciting but ensure they are creditworthy before you commit time and resources to working with them.

- Agree terms in advance. Agree terms of payment with new clients as part of the sales process. Make sure they understand that the price of your services are linked to the credit terms you offer and make it crystal clear that you have a legal right to claim interest.
- Inform your debtors. If you have habitual late payers, contact them and explain how the latest legislation could affect them. Try to foster good working relationships with your clients and suppliers so that it's easier to resolve payment problems when they arise.

  Say, for example, you purchase a new wide screen TV on credit. What would happen if you did not make your credit payments on time? Why should things be any different for your clients who do not pay on time?
- Send out invoices as you have sent your translation to your client. Do not delay sending invoices out. If you don't do this you can't expect to be paid on time.
- Keep clear documentation. Make sure you send accurate invoices/statements to the right person, at the right place, at the right time and state clearly the date payment is due.
- Understand your rights. The law gives you, as a small firm, the right to charge interest on all late payments owed to you. In the United Kingdom the amount you can charge is the Bank of England Base Rate plus eight per cent.
- Collect your money on time. Have a collection timetable and stick to it. If a promised cheque fails to arrive, chase it again straight away.
- Communicate effectively. Ensure that existing clients are quickly made aware of any due invoices. Re-check the creditworthiness of any client who continues to withhold payment.
- If you work for an agency, your contract is with that agency and not with the agency's client. The agency has no right to delay payment because the agency's client has not settled his account.
- Have the right attitude. Don't be embarrassed about discussing money. Are you offended when a supplier runs a credit check on you when you make a purchase?

9.8   Procedure for dealing with client disputes

Quality control of your work covers not only the translation but all the procedures you apply to your work. Accountability is very important, particularly if a matter of dispute is referred to a third person for arbitration or apportionment of liability. Proper and comprehensive documentation of all phases in the production of a translation is para-mount. All relevant information for producing a translation according to a client's requirements must be entered on the records you keep. **Incomplete or illegible infor-mation is quite unacceptable**. Correct documentation will allow you to trace where any faults occurred or where any limitations lie. Reference to an undocumented telephone conversation is not a particularly powerful argument in a dispute.

It is realistic to expect that, on the odd occasion, there will be a dispute with a client. Though it is never our intention that a client will have cause to dispute the quality of the work provided, we must be aware of the factors that could lead to dispute and what remedial action can be taken. An awareness of what problems can arise heightens preparedness to deal with such problems or prevent their recurrence.

The following are possible reasons for dissatisfaction or dispute.

1. The work was not received by the client in time.
2. The translation is (supposedly) incorrect or the wrong terminology is used.
3. The translated text is incomplete.
4. The style of the translation is not suitable for the intended purpose.
5. The layout of the translation was not provided according to the client's specifications.
6. The translation was not provided in the correct software format.

Flowcharts showing how to deal with disputes caused by the above are shown at the end of this chapter.

All occurrences should be recorded and filed, as should the action taken and the outcome of the dispute. If necessary, a report can be sent to the client giving factual explanations. Transparent excuses are not acceptable. I know this increases the amount of administration, but keeping comprehensive records can be worth the effort when trying to resolve a dispute perhaps months after you have completed a translation and are still trying to get paid.

The generally considered opinion is that a translator can achieve an output of around 2,000 words a day. The time required for checking depends on the quality of the translation and its intended purpose, and must be added to the translation time.

It may be necessary for the translation to be split between several translators and then checked/edited to ensure uniformity. The client must be informed if this option is selected.

9.9 Arbitration

If a dispute with a client cannot be resolved by discussion, and you consider that you have acted correctly, you can refer the matter of the dispute to one of the professional associations (assuming you are a member) or your insurance brokers as soon as you suspect that a dispute might become a reality. You should have this arbitration condition stated in your terms of business. The ITI (The Institute of Translation and Interpreting) is used in the flowcharts that follow.

If arbitration judges in favour of the client, the matter will then be referred to your indemnity insurance brokers for possible compensation. *If the value of the claim is less than your insurance excess, you may consider settling directly with the client if this is considered appropriate.* The insurance company will pay compensation accordingly (less your excess, of course). If the source of the dispute lies with a freelance translator to whom you have sub-contracted work, compensation will be claimed against him by you or your insurance company.

If arbitration judges in favour of you, you need to act diplomatically and try to retain the client's confidence and future business. It is however likely that if a matter goes as far as arbitration, client confidence may have been eroded and he may go elsewhere.

The following flowcharts allow you to analyse where a fault lies and what action to take. These will hopefully allow you to resolve the matter without having to go to arbitration. If you cannot resolve the issue directly with the client then arbitration is the only realistic option you have open to you. Keep in close contact with your insurance broker throughout since he can often act as a mediator between you and your client.

The flowcharts (in part) are applicable to individual translators but cover most of the steps through which a translation goes on its road to completion. 'Agency' in the flowcharts is the translation agency/company (or even individual translator dealing directly with a client and who sub-contracts work to other translators) who accepts a translation assignment. 'Translator' refers to either a staff translator or freelancer who carries out work on behalf of the agency/company (or individual translator).

The following is an instruction that was used in my former company's Quality Manual and illustrates the steps that can be taken to resolve a client complaint in an equitable manner.

Client Complaints

DOCUMENT HISTORY

Nature of amendment	Date	Signature
Originator	11 September 1996	GSB
Date of approval for general distribution of Issue A	06 August 1997	GSB
Amended subsequent to organisation changes.Header amended to denote Controlled Copy.	08 January 1998	GSB

This instruction comprises a flowchart that extends over three pages and illustrates how client complaints are handled from receipt to resolution.

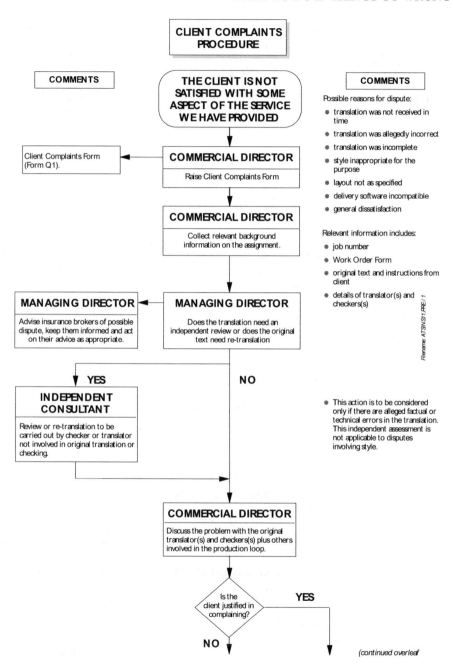

CLIENT COMPLAINTS PROCEDURE

THE CLIENT IS NOT SATISFIED WITH SOME ASPECT OF THE SERVICE WE HAVE PROVIDED

COMMENTS

COMMENTS

Client Complaints Form (Form Q1).

COMMERCIAL DIRECTOR

Raise Client Complaints Form

Possible reasons for dispute:

- translation was not received in time
- translation was allegedly incorrect
- translation was incomplete
- style inappropriate for the purpose
- layout not as specified
- delivery software incompatible
- general dissatisfaction

COMMERCIAL DIRECTOR

Collect relevant background information on the assignment.

Relevant information includes:

- job number
- Work Order Form
- original text and instructions from client
- details of translator(s) and checkers(s)

Filename: ATS/NS1.PRE/1

MANAGING DIRECTOR

Advise insurance brokers of possible dispute, keep them informed and act on their advice as appropriate.

MANAGING DIRECTOR

Does the translation need an independent review or does the original text need re-translation

YES   NO

INDEPENDENT CONSULTANT

Review or re-translation to be carried out by checker or translator not involved in original translation or checking.

- This action is to be considered only if there are alleged factual or technical errors in the translation. This independent assessment is not applicable to disputes involving style.

COMMERCIAL DIRECTOR

Discuss the problem with the original translator(s) and checkers(s) plus others involved in the production loop.

Is the client justified in complaining?   YES

NO   (continued overleaf

135

A PRACTICAL GUIDE FOR TRANSLATORS

Flowchart continued from page 2.

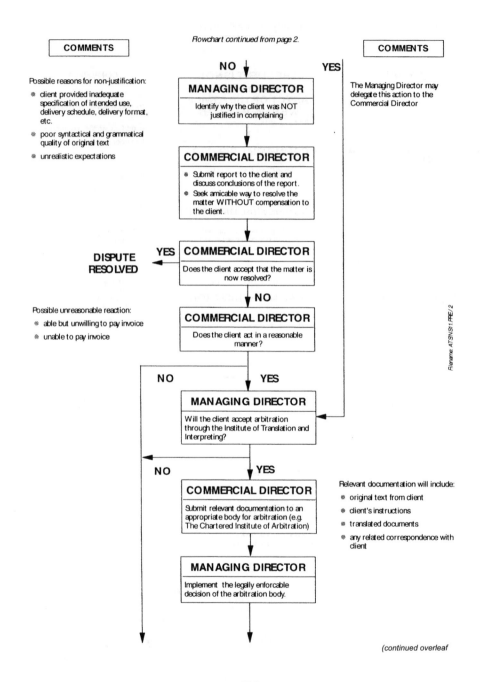

COMMENTS

Possible reasons for non-justification:

* client provided inadequate specification of intended use, delivery schedule, delivery format, etc.

* poor syntactical and grammatical quality of original text

* unrealistic expectations

NO ↓

MANAGING DIRECTOR

Identify why the client was NOT justified in complaining

COMMENTS

The Managing Director may delegate this action to the Commercial Director

COMMERCIAL DIRECTOR

* Submit report to the client and discuss conclusions of the report.
* Seek amicable way to resolve the matter WITHOUT compensation to the client.

DISPUTE RESOLVED ← **YES**

COMMERCIAL DIRECTOR

Does the client accept that the matter is now resolved?

NO

COMMERCIAL DIRECTOR

Does the client act in a reasonable manner?

Possible unreasonable reaction:

* able but unwilling to pay invoice
* unable to pay invoice

NO   **YES**

MANAGING DIRECTOR

Will the client accept arbitration through the Institute of Translation and Interpreting?

NO   **YES**

COMMERCIAL DIRECTOR

Submit relevant documentation to an appropriate body for arbitration (e.g. The Chartered Institute of Arbitration)

Relevant documentation will include:

* original text from client
* client's instructions
* translated documents
* any related correspondence with client

MANAGING DIRECTOR

Implement the legally enforcable decision of the arbitration body.

Filename ATSNS1.PRE/2

(continued overleaf

136

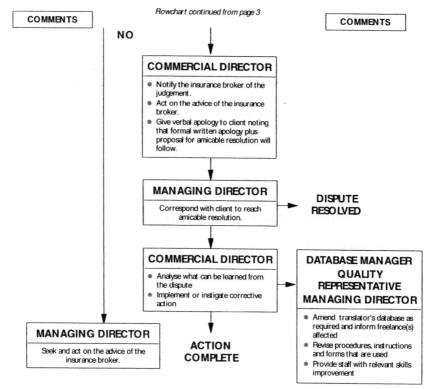

Flowchart continued from page 3

COMMENTS

COMMENTS

NO

COMMERCIAL DIRECTOR
* Notify the insurance broker of the judgement.
* Act on the advice of the insurance broker.
* Give verbal apology to client noting that formal written apology plus proposal for amicable resolution will follow.

MANAGING DIRECTOR
Correspond with client to reach amicable resolution.

DISPUTE RESOLVED

COMMERCIAL DIRECTOR
* Analyse what can be learned from the dispute
* Implement or instigate corrective action

DATABASE MANAGER QUALITY REPRESENTATIVE MANAGING DIRECTOR
* Amend translator's database as required and inform freelance(s) affected
* Revise procedures, instructions and forms that are used
* Provide staff with relevant skills improvement

MANAGING DIRECTOR
Seek and act on the advice of the insurance broker.

ACTION COMPLETE

Filename: ATS/NS1.PRE/3

137

10 Professional organisations for translators

'Translation is at best an echo.'
George Borrow, 1803–1881

10.1 Fédération Internationale des Traducteurs (FIT)

As the title suggests, FIT is the international organisation which elects national organisations for membership. The FIT was founded in Paris in 1953 and has member associations in over 50 countries world-wide. Through its 77 full member associations and 24 associate member associations, FIT represents the interests of over 100,000 translators. FIT is a strictly non-political organisation which enjoys category A status with UNESCO. It plays a vital role in overcoming language barriers and promoting world-wide understanding.

For up-to-date information refer to FIT's website on www.fit-ift.org.

10.1.1 Objectives

FIT has the following as its principal objectives:

a) to bring together associations of translators and to promote interaction and cooperation between such associations;

b) to sponsor and facilitate the formation of such associations in countries where they do not already exist;

c) to establish links with other organisations devoted to translation or other aspects of interlingual and intercultural communication;

d) to develop among all member organisations such harmony and understanding as will promote the interests of translators, and offer support, whenever desirable or necessary, in resolving any differences that may arise between the various organisations;

e) to provide member organisations with such information and advice as may be useful to them;

f)   to promote training and research;
g)   to promote the harmonisation of professional standards;
h)   and, generally, to uphold the moral and material interests of translators throughout the world, advocate and advance the recognition of their profession, enhance their status in society and further the knowledge and appreciation of translation as a science and an art.

10.1.2 Central issues

Through its special committees, FIT endeavours to meet the needs of members through-out the world by addressing such issues as training, working conditions and recognition of the profession. The UNESCO recommendation on the Protection and Improvement of the Legal and Social Status of Translations and Translators, adopted in Nairobi in 1976, is a milestone in the history of FIT. FIT is proud of its achievements on behalf of the translating profession.

At the same time, it is well aware of the work that remains to be done to meet the growing demand for international communication and co-operation, FIT, therefore, continues to play its vital role in overcoming the language barriers and in promoting worldwide understanding.

10.1.3 FIT prizes

The FIT awards a number of prizes. Brief details are given in the following and full details can be obtained from FIT's website. The rules for awarding these prizes were approved by the FIT Council at its meeting in Geneva in April 1998.

The Astrid Lindgren Translation Prize

This prize is designed to promote the translation of children's literature, improve the quality thereof and draw attention to the role of translators in bringing the peoples of the world closer together in terms of culture. The prize is sponsored by the Astrid Lindgren Fund, based on a generous donation made by the author herself.

The prize may be awarded either for a single translation of outstanding quality or for the entire body of work of a translator of books written for children or young people. It is at FIT World Congresses, pursuant to the decision of an international jury.

The Prize consists of a Certificate of Merit and a sum of money.

The Pierre-François Caillé Memorial Medal

Pierre-François Caillé was the founder of FIT. The Pierre-François Caillé Memorial Medal is intended to provide recognition to individuals who have demonstrated exceptional merit in promoting the status and reputation of the translation profession at the international level.

The medal may be awarded at FIT World Congresses although the jury is not required to make the award at every World Congress. The recipient of the Pierre-François Caillé Memorial Medal must be a member in good standing of a FIT member.

The Karel Capek Medal

This international translation award is designed to promote the translation of literary works written in languages of limited diffusion. The objectives of the award are to improve the quality of such literary translations and to draw attention to the role of translators in bringing the peoples of the world closer together in terms of culture.

Karel Capek was a famous Czech author of fiction and non-fiction literature. The Karel Capek Medal was presented for the first time at the XIIth FIT Congress in 1990, on the occasion of the 100th anniversary of Karel Capek's birth, which is observed as a UNESCO anniversary. The Medal may be awarded either for a single translation of outstanding quality or for the entire body of work of a literary translator of books written in languages of limited diffusion.

This medal may be awarded at FIT World Congresses pursuant to the decision of an international jury. This is an honorary prize consisting of a Certificate of Merit and Medal bearing a likeness of Karel Capek (provided by the Czech Translators' Association).

The FIT prize for best periodical

The competition is open to any journal published by any FIT member, or any recognised branch, chapter, regional group or section of such organisation. It takes place during the FIT World Congress.

A Certificate of Merit is awarded to the journal which is considered to best promote the professional image of the translator and/or interpreter in terms of quality, presentation and relevance. The jury may also decide that one or more of the other nominations deserves honourable mention.

The FIT Aurora Borealis prize for outstanding translation of non-fiction literature

This international translation prize is designed to promote the translation of non-fiction literature, improve the quality thereof and draw attention to the role of translators in bringing the peoples of the world closer together in terms of culture. The prize is sponsored by a generous donation from the Norwegian Association of Non-fiction Writers and Translators (NFF), and is financed by copyright revenues.

This international translation prize may be awarded either for a single translation of outstanding quality or for the entire body of a translator's non-fiction work. It is awarded at FIT World Congresses, pursuant to the decision of an international jury. The prize consists of a Certificate of Merit and a sum of money.

The FIT Aurora Borealis Prize for outstanding translation of fiction literature

This international translation prize is designed to promote the translation of non-fiction literature, improve the quality thereof and draw attention to the role of translators in bringing the peoples of the world closer together in terms of culture. The prize is sponsored by a generous donation from the Norwegian Association of Fiction Writers and Translators (NO), and is financed by copyright revenues.

This international translation prize may be awarded either for a single translation of outstanding quality or for the entire body of a translator's fiction work. It is awarded at FIT World Congresses, pursuant to the decision of an international jury.

The Prize consists of a Certificate of Merit and a sum of money.

FIT World Congresses

FIT holds its World Congress every three years when, in addition its statutory congress being held, translators present papers, attend workshops and take the opportunity to meet colleagues and other translators from all parts of the world.

The following illustrates the structure of FIT and its member organisations. Note that membership does not extend to commercial organisations such as translation agencies.

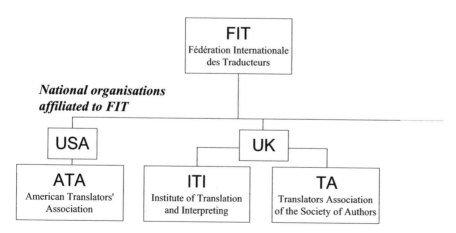

Figure 18. International structure of translator organisations

10.2 Professional organisations for translators in the United Kingdom

By referring only to translation organisations in the United Kingdom I am aware that this exposes me to the accusation of being ethnocentric. However, these are the only organisations, apart from the FIT, of which I have first hand experience. If you go to the FIT website you can find out about all the member translation organisations in different countries.

There are three professional organisations for translators in the United Kingdom. Two of them, the Institute of Linguists and the Institute of Translation and Interpreting, award recognised professional qualifications after careful assessment or examination. This allows suitably-qualified people to use designations such as Dip.Trans., MIL or MITI to denote a level of achievement. Let's look at each of the three organisations in detail.

10.2.1 The Institute of Linguists

The Institute of Linguists (IoL) was founded in 1910 to serve the interests of all professional linguists. It currently has around 6,400 Fellows, Members and Associate members. The divisional membership in late 2002 is shown in the figure below. Note that members may belong to more than one division and that some members choose not to be a member of any division.

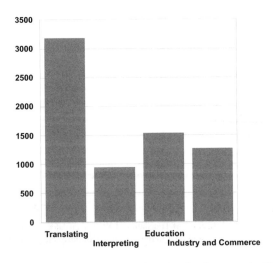

Figure 19.   Analysis of IoL membership by divisional affiliation

The IoL is the largest professional body for linguists in the United Kingdom and has extensive links abroad. IoL membership was for many years biased towards those in academic professions but has recently become more business-orientated. It went through major changes in its structure in the middle of the 1980s.

Aims and objectives

The IoL has a number of distinct aims and objectives. The Institute's aims are:

- To promote proficiency in the use of languages used by professional linguists and those who use languages in industry, commerce and public services.
- To set and improve national standards of language competence.
- To provide a range of language examinations for educational, vocational and professional purposes.
- To provide services to its members.
- To promote general awareness of the importance of languages and recognition of the professional status of linguists.
- To provide advice and guidance on language issues.

These aims are supported by a number of business objectives:

- To increase membership world-wide (including corporate, affiliate and student members).
- To increase the number of IoL examination candidates world-wide.
- To provide referrals for members.
- To increase the use of the Language Services Unit involving members wherever possible.
- To take a more active lobbying role in the UK, Europe and internationally.
- To expand language services contracts with government departments and Brussels.

Membership benefits

The IoL provides language qualifications of recognised standing. Membership benefits include regional societies and specialist divisions, receiving the Institute's journal *The Linguist* and access to an extensive library.

Members have the opportunity to join any of the Institute's Divisions which cater for specialist interests. These divisions are the Education Division, the Industry and Commerce Division, the Translating Division and the Interpreting Division. The Divisions offer programmes of interest to newcomers to the professions and to established linguists. With its network of contact groups, the Translating Division is the largest body for translators in the UK. Members may also join the Institute's Regional Societies in most parts of the UK, including Scotland and Northern Ireland, and a number of countries abroad. They offer a varied programme of relevance to linguists everywhere.

The Institute has much to offer to undergraduates on language degree courses and recent language graduates. Joining the Institute as a student member or Affiliate provides membership of a highly professional body including linguists working not only as translators and interpreters but in marketing, insurance, international banking, the Civil Service or the EU.

There are five grades of individual membership, three of which are denoted by letters after the member's name. These are: Fellow (FIL), Member (MIL), Associate (AIL), Affiliate and Registered Student. Only the first three denote any professional achievement. The use of Affiliate in advertising is not permitted since, to the uninitiated, it may give the impression that the user has achieved a level of linguistic standing. Commercial companies, teaching and other institutions and professional bodies may apply for corporate membership.

Like most professional bodies, the IoL has a Code of Professional Conduct and its members are subject to the disciplinary procedures of the Institute. Fortunately, they are hardly ever needed as cases of genuine grievance are rare.

The Institute of Linguists is also a leading examinations body. Its most up-to-date syllabus, Examinations in Languages for International Communication (ELIC) has been widely acclaimed as a benchmark in modern language testing. The examinations range from beginners to post graduate/professional level. The Diploma in Translation is widely accepted as the entrance qualification into the translation profession. Examinations in less-commonly taught languages and public service interpreting are also available, as well as the Diploma in English and Chinese.

The Institute provides a range of public examinations and also conducts examinations for the Home Office Departments, the Ministry of Defence and other specialist users. The Institute's public examinations are qualifications of practical and vocational linguistic skills. Examinations are available in over 100 languages.

Membership of the IoL (MIL) is widely accepted as degree qualification for teachers. Institute qualifications and membership are recognised internationally. The IoL now publishes a comprehensive Directory and List of Members.

Diploma in Public Service Interpreting

The Institute offers the only vocational interpreting qualification for public service interpreters, currently available in the UK. The Diploma in Public Service Interpreting is set in three specialised contexts: the legal, health and local government fields within the UK. This qualification is set at a language level equivalent to degree standard and is the principal entry qualification to the National Register of Public Service Interpreters.

The National Register is administered by the Institute of Linguists on behalf of the Lord Chancellor's Department and of the Home Office. It is the only single database covering all of the UK which provides details of interpreters who are qualified and experienced to work at a professional level within the public services, and who have been vetted by the Institute.

Diploma in Translation

The Diploma in Translation is a professional qualification intended for working translators and for those who, having reached a high level of linguistic competence, wish to embark on a career in professional translation. It is available to candidates with a level of linguistic competence at least equivalent to a good Honours degree in languages.

Successful candidates are entitled to use the designation 'Dip Trans'. On provision of evidence of oral competence, they are also eligible to apply for full membership of the Institute.

The Diploma tests the ability of candidates to translate to a professional standard, together with their awareness of the professional task of the translator. The passages set for translation are of the standard of difficulty that translators would expect to meet in their daily work. They are not however of an over-technical or specialised nature.

Candidates are emphatically advised that full professional competence is normally achieved only by translators working into their mother tongue or language of habitual use. English is usually either the source or the target language for this Diploma. Other language combinations are coming on stream.

National Vocational Qualifications

The Institute of Linguists is the accredited awarding body for the National Vocational Qualification Level 5 in Interpreting (for spoken languages). This NVQ, which provides an alternative access route to the National Register of Public Service Interpreters, is currently being piloted and will be publicly available in 1999.

The Institute has also submitted an application for accreditation as the awarding body for the NVQ Level 5 in Translation.

10.2.2 Institute of Linguist prizes

The Institute awards a number of trophies and prizes in several categories.

ELIC: Examinations in Languages for International Communication

Threlford Memorial Cup: donated by the Institute's Founder, Sir Lacon Threlford, for the best performing college in the ELIC examinations.

Deakin Rose Bowl: for the next college with the best results in the ELIC examinations.

Youhotsky Cup: for the best candidate in the ELIC Russian Final Diploma Module 1.

Cozens Elliot Trophy: for the best candidate in the ELIC Diploma Module 1 examination in Portuguese.

Follick Cup: for the best candidate in the ELIC English Background Knowledge paper.
Middleton Cup: for the best candidate in the ELIC Intermediate level in Spanish.

Diploma in Translation

Richard Lewis Trophy: for the candidate with the best overall performance in the Diploma in Translation.
Schlapps Oliver Shield: for the best overall performance from a group entry in the Diploma in Translation.

Bilingual Skills Certificate

Finlay Trophy: for the candidate who achieves the best results in the Bilingual Skills Certificate in any language.

Diploma in Public Service Interpreting (DPSI)

The Nuffield Prize is awarded for the candidate who achieves the best results in the Diploma in Public Services Interpreting.

Other membership benefits

The Institute's bi-monthly journal, *The Linguist*, keeps members up to date in every way. It contains special features and regular information on technology for translators.

The Institute's library, based at Regent's College, Central London, has over three thousand volumes of specialist and technical dictionaries. A member of the Institute's staff is available one afternoon each week to help members with their inquiries.

The Institute plays a major role in the world of languages and worked closely with the Languages Lead Body and has established national language standards.

For more information about the Institute of Linguists contact:

Institute of Linguists
Saxon House
48 Southwark Street
London SE1 1UN
Telephone: 020 7940 3100
www.iol.org.uk

Website

The website of the Institute of Linguists functions as both an information source for general enquirers, and a focal point for its network of professional members. The world-wide web enables the Institute to publicise its services as a languages membership and examining body to potential members both in the UK and internationally, and to facilitate discussion and information exchange between members through its linguists' forum. The on-line 'Find a Linguist' service will provide an invaluable service in bringing the expertise of the Institute's members to the attention of organisations and individuals in need of a translator, interpreter, tutor or other language professional.

10.3 The Institute of Translation and Interpreting

The Institute of Translation and Interpreting, or the ITI as it is more popularly known, was founded in 1986. Its founding was in response to an overwhelming demand from everyone concerned with the quality of translating and interpreting in industry, commerce, literature, science, research, law and administration.

The ITI's main aim is to promote the highest standards in a profession where the specialist is fast replacing the general linguist. It serves as a forum for all those who understand the importance of translation and interpreting to the economy, especially with the advent of the single European market.

The ITI is involved in translator and interpreting training at universities and colleges, and runs its own programme of in-career training sessions. It offers guidance to those who wish to enter the profession, as well as advice to those who provide translations, and to potential employers and clients. It keeps in close contact with the producers of equipment, software, databanks and dictionaries. The ITI is the primary source of information to government, industry, the media and the general public in all matters relating to translation and interpreting.

The ITI has been elected by the Fédération Internationale des Traducteurs (FIT) as one of the two UK voting members, and maintains close contacts with sister organisations world-wide. A member of the ITI is at present on the Council and Executive Bureau of FIT, to make sure that the UK plays an influential part in its activities.

The ITI does not act as an agency, but provides names of suitable linguists and translation agencies in response to enquiries. It offers a consultancy service to help assess language requirements, and an arbitration service in the event of complaints. It also has a professional standards body to consider any alleged breaches of professional ethics by its members.

The governing body of the ITI is its Council which is so constituted that practising translators and interpreters will always form a majority over all other categories of members.

10.3.1 Membership

The ITI has around 2000 members. Those who are suitable qualified and have satisfied the Admissions Committee as to their professional competence and experience are listed in the ITI Directory. Such members are entitled to use the designation MITI. AITIs (Associates) are members who require additional formal work experience and are listed in a separate section of the directory. Fellows (FITI), students, subscribers and corporate members make up the remaining membership.

Membership categories

Student

Student membership is open to:

- anybody attending a full time undergraduate course with a major component of languages in the United Kingdom or overseas
- anybody studying translation or interpreting full time overseas
- anybody attending a full time or part time translation or interpreting course at post-graduate level.

No person may remain a student member for more than four years or for one calendar year after completing the relevant course of study.

Associate

The requirements for admission to Associate membership are all of the following requirements and not just one of them:

1. a minimum age of 21 years,
2. a first degree in a relevant subject or a corresponding qualification accepted by the Council,
3. recommendation regarding ability, volume of work and good repute by at least two persons for translators and three for interpreters,
4. recent professional experience:
   a) for translators, a minimum of one year full time – considered to be in the region of 300,000 words of translation – or a corresponding period of part time experience;
   b) for interpreters, a minimum of 100 days interpreting.

A translator or interpreter may remain an Associate without limit of time.
An Associate is entitled to use the designation AITI after his name.

Member

The requirements for admission to Qualified membership are all of the following requirements and not just one of them:

1. a minimum age of 25 years,
2. a first degree or postgraduate qualification in a relevant subject or a corresponding qualification accepted by the Council,
3. recommendation regarding ability, volume of work and good repute by at least two persons for translators and three for *ad hoc* interpreters or five for conference inter-preters,

4. recent professional experience:
   a) for translators, a minimum of five years full time – considered to be in the region of 300,000 words of translation per year- or a corresponding period of part time experience – and successful assessment of work; alternatively three years' full time (or a corresponding longer period of part time) plus a pass in the ITI Membership examination, unless the applicant can satisfy the Admissions Committee that there are exceptional grounds for exception;
   b) for interpreters, a minimum of 200 days interpreting over a period of five years, or a minimum of 120 days over a period of three years plus a pass in the ITI Interpreters' Examination.

A Member is entitled to use the designation MITI after his name.

Fellow
This is an honorary grade and cannot be applied for.

A Member who has a minimum of ten years' full time (or a correspondingly longer period of part time) professional experience may be admitted by the ITI Council as a Fellow. The number of Fellows in the ITI shall at no time exceed one-tenth of the total number of qualified members.

A Fellow is entitled to use the designation FITI after his name.

Corporate membership
Corporate membership is open to higher education establishments, professional and research associations, translation companies, publishers, industrial and commercial bodies, government departments and non-governmental organisations and others concerned with the quality of translation and interpreting.

Subscriber status
Any individual showing evidence of interest in translation or interpreting as a profession may be admitted as a Subscriber without limit of eligibility or duration.

Terms and Conditions

A set of terms and conditions governing the way you work, and your relationship with a client is very much advisable. The ITI has produced such a document which can provide a very useful guide when formulating your own terms of business.

Code of Conduct

The ITI has produced a Code of Conduct that has been approved by the Office of Fair Trading.

ITI Publications

The Institute publishes an annually updated, comprehensive Directory of qualified members. This directory is available to all users of translating and interpreting services. Members are listed under language and subject headings, with their address, telephone, electronic communications and equipment details. This is available online at the ITI's website, on CD-ROM and in printed form.

The ITI Bulletin appears bi-monthly and contains feature articles and regular contributions from professionals all over the world. It also acts as a channel for informative, practical communication between members and provides details of forthcoming events.

In addition to these regular publications, the ITI publishes a range of leaflets and pamphlets on various topics that are available for the guidance of translators and interpreters whether they be new to the profession or well established. Details are available from the Secretariat.

Certification of translations

As a professional association, one that assesses the quality of its members, maintains a list of its members with suitable language skills and technical expertise, and can hold its members to account in the event of complaints, the ITI has taken steps to establish itself as a body whose members can certify translations. To ensure that certified translations are accurate and of good quality:

- an MITI or FITI may certify a translation if the translation has been produced by himself It is desirable to have the translation checked by a second MITI, FITI or corporate member. In other words, every certified translation should be verified wherever possible;
- an AITI, MITI or FITI may produce a translation for certification, subject to the ITI's code of ethics (mother tongue rule, within the person's own subject field etc.);
- the certificate should be on the certifier's headed paper, identify the translator and be firmly attached to a photocopy of the original and the original translation by stitching and sealing with the ITI certification seal. The certifier should sign or initial each page of each attachment.

Background – sworn translations, not sworn translators

In the common law system that exists in England, we do not have the status of 'sworn translator' that exists in civil law countries.

Even so, translations need to be 'sworn' or certified for various purposes. Certifying or swearing has no bearing on the quality of the translation but serves to identify the translator and his qualifications so that he is accountable.

When a translation is sworn before a solicitor, the solicitor does not verify the quality of the translation but merely satisfies himself as to the translator's identity. Certification does, however, lend weight to a translation. If, for example, a document is wilfully mistranslated or carelessly translated, the translator could be held charged with contempt of court, perjury or negligence.

Acceptability of ITI certification by the authorities

The legal advice taken by the ITI is that 'a certificate is acceptable if it is accepted' and that we as suitably qualified translators should certify translations and wait to see whether such a certificate is challenged and, if so, by whom. The ITI's advisors feel that such a challenge is unlikely or, that by the time a challenge does arise, a firm precedent will have been set. To my knowledge, only one challenge has been made against ITI certification since the scheme has been in operation.

When users of translations insist on a higher grade of certification, they should be reminded of the existence of notarisation and referred to notaries (and where practicable to firms whose members are ITI members). Comprehensive details are given in guidelines issued by the ITI.

Example certification

A scanned example of certification is given on the next page.

The wording of the certification should be as follows:

I, the undersigned, *[Name]*, Fellow/Member of the Institute of Translation and Interpreting, *[other qualifications]* declare that the translation of the attached document(s) *[identifying particulars]* is, to the best of my knowledge and belief, a true and faithful rendering of the original *[language]*, done to the best of my ability as a professional translator *[and verified by (name and ITI membership qualification)]*

[Signature]

Attachments:

A1. Document (brief identification)
A2. Translation of A1
B1. Document (brief identification)
B2. Translation of B1
. . . etc.

● 100 Northcott, Bracknell, Berkshire RG12 7WS, United Kingdom ● Website: www.gsbconsulting.co.uk ● Email: info@gsbconsulting.co.uk
● Tel: +44 (0)1344 319570 ● Fax: +44 (0)1344 319571 ● Mobile: +44 (0)771 8900431

> To whom it may concern

Reference: 1286
Date: 12 September 2002

CERTIFICATION

I, the undersigned, Geoffrey Francis Samuelsson-Brown, DipTrans IoL, Fellow of the Institute of Linguists, Fellow of the Institute of Translation and Interpreting, and Member of the Swedish Association of Professional Translators, having a knowledge of the Danish and English languages, declare that the translations of the attached documents from Danish into English are, to the best of my knowledge and belief, a true and faithful rendering of the original.

While every effort has been made to ensure accuracy in translation, the original Danish document takes precedence over the translation in the event of any dispute concerning interpretation.

<u>Attachments (with each page identified by the company stamp and my initials):</u>

Translation from Danish into English (2 pages)

Danish documents provided as photocopies for translation (2 pages)

Dated Bracknell, 12 September 2002

Signature

....

Geoffrey Samuelsson-Brown
MBA FIL FITI DipTrans DipMgmt MCMI MIoD

ISO 9002

Certificate No: 11078

10.3.2 ITI Prizes

The John Hayes Memorial Prize

This prize, which comprises a book token, is awarded to the successful Membership examination candidate who achieves the best examination results.

The John Sykes Memorial Award

This is a recently institute prize and details had not been provided at the time of going to press.

10.3.3 Contact details

The Institute of Translation and Interpreting
Fortuna House
South Fifth Street
Milton Keynes
MK9 2EU
Telephone: 01908 325250

More details visit ITI's website at www.iti.org.uk.

10.4 The Translators Association

The Translators Association – TA – is a subsidiary group with the Society of Authors and was formed in 1958. Its aim is to provide support for translators of published works, and to promote the highest standards of literary translation. Translators who are members of the TA are, for the most part, literary translators. Through membership of the TA, translators who work alone in a wide variety of circumstances can obtain support and advice concerning the business aspects of literary translation.

Prior to 1958, the absence of a representative organisation contributed, without any doubt, to the fact that translators were among the least considered and lowest paid of professional writers. They were under constant pressure to either accept a low level of income, or to speed up their work to the detriment of quality. For that reason the TA began by giving help to the translators of books but it has extended assistance to include translators working in other media.

Much has been accomplished. The TA has worked hard and with marked success to raise the status of the profession and to increase rates of remuneration to their present level. It has campaigned steadily to ensure that translators receive proper credits for their work and improved terms of contract with publishers. The membership has risen steadily since 1958. This is already an achievement but it is in everybody's interest that the TA has a strong membership since the stronger the voice of its membership the better the TA can represent the profession.

The TA is affiliated to the Fédération Internationale des Traducteurs. The TA is also a member of the Conseil Européen des Associations de Traducteurs Littéraires (CEATL).

10.4.1 Translators and copyright

Entire books and innumerable papers have been written on the subject of translators and copyright. Since the TA, and others, have devoted considerable time and energy to this subject, I feel it appropriate to bring up the question at this juncture. Literary translators are also more likely to be concerned with copyright.

Many FIT members spend a great deal of time discussing the legal status of the *translator* without taking as their starting point the legal status of the *translation*. Copyright Law is an international phenomenon and what it says about translation deserves to be taken seriously. All the European countries, and most other developed countries in the world, have signed the international treaty known as the Berne Convention, so it is reasonable to consider what this Convention states. Article 1 of the Convention starts off by giving cross-border protection to what it calls 'literary works' and, under Article 2 of the Convention goes on to define the meaning of 'literary works'.

It is clear from the definition that the word 'literary' is a technical term not containing any value judgement. It does not refer only to works that have some kind of high cultural value or that are soaring products of the imagination. All kinds of written and spoken material are included. The Article then states quite unambiguously that '*translations . . . and other alterations of literary work shall be protected as original works*'.

For translators this principal of copyright protection is of huge importance. It effect being that, when the translator is asked to make a translation, the translator is not being engaged to 'do a job' like a worker who is hired to paint a wall or upholster a chair. The translator is being asked to create an 'original work' in which he is the owner of the copyright.

For translators of novels, poetry and plays this is not a difficult concept. It is easy for all to see that translations of such works are not a copy or a straight conversion of the original foreign language work. To produce a faithful and readable translation, the translator must write creatively in the target language and the result is better described as an adaptation than a copy. In the theatre, too, we are used to seeing a succession of new translations of the same classic plays by Ibsen, Chekhov or whoever. They are designed to be appreciated by different audiences and are sufficiently distinct from each other for it to be clear that each translator has created an 'original work'.

Since the law says that the translator is the owner of the copyright in the translation, it places the translator in the position of being able to grant licences for specific rights to the material. For instance, the translator of a novel may grant an exclusive licence for a publisher to issue a printed edition of the translation in hardcover in return for an advance payment on account of royalties. In addition, the publisher may be asked to pass on a share of the receipts from the serialisation of the work, from a bookclub edition, from a paperback reprint, and so on.

Dividing the 'copyright' into a number of different 'rights' in this way produces, in the end, a greater income for the translator. It also conforms with the 1976 Nairobi Recommendations of UNESCO which stipulate that a translator is entitled to receive payment in relation to the extent to which his work is exploited. These Recommendations conform only to what was present in the Berne Convention: that a translator's business should be conducted on the same footing as the business of the original author of a literary work.

By defining the legal status of the *translation*, therefore, Copyright Law establishes the legal status of the *translator*. The status is that of a creative artist and not that of an artisan. Furthermore, the copyright legislation of virtually all European countries now includes what are called 'moral rights' for the translator. The Right of Integrity ensures that the translator's work may not be used in a derogatory fashion; and the Right of Paternity (which has to be asserted in writing in the UK but which is automatic in many other countries) ensures that when it is published, the translation must always bear the translator's name. These moral rights, it could be said, establish that the translator is an individual with human rights instead of an anonymous and faceless entity.

This support for status and pride of the 'literary translator' is all very well but is Copyright Law of any practical value to translators of business reports, instruction manuals, conference proceedings, etc? The answer is yes, whenever the translator is working on a freelance basis and not producing translations in the course of employment. There may be greater difficulty in recognising that a work of non-fiction (what in French is confusingly called *non-littéraire*) is an original literary work that is entitled to copyright protection. It may even be harder not to look upon a translation of a short item as being more in the nature of 'a job'. This is especially the case if the assignment is the translation of a matter-of-fact business report or an instruction booklet for a piece of kitchen equipment. Nevertheless, these translations still qualify as copyright works under the Berne Convention and also under national copyright legislation. Even the instructions on a bottle of pills can, conceivably, be treated in different, i.e. creative ways. Consider the following: 'To be taken three times a day after meals', or 'Take three tablets a day after food', or 'One tablet to be taken after each meal thrice daily'.

Translators of technical and commercial material who allow themselves to be paid in the form of a lump sum for 'doing a job' actually encourage a false perception of the translator as an anonymous, robotic casual worker, lacking in individual creativity; not only with a low status but with no hope of a proper career structure. Literary translators tend to feel in their hearts (though they may not say it to their non-literary colleagues' faces) that such translators let the side down.

Translation ought to be a profession with the same standing and career prospects as, say, the medical profession or the legal profession or, closer to home, the (original) writing profession. Translators long to be awarded the recognition they deserve and to have a real opportunity to be rewarded on merit in the same way as best-selling and well-loved authors. Instead, the jobbing translators often seem to drag down their colleagues by conditioning the people who commission translations into thinking that a one-off lump sum payment is the norm, even when they are commissioning is the most exquisite creative translation of a great work of literature. Translation agencies are in an invidious position since, in a market economy and trying to operate like a service industry, they do not or are unable to assert the individuality of the translator.

Not every translator will eventually translate a Chekhov play but, in the course of their lives, most will produce a small number of translations that are going to be used not only once but again and again in different forms, in different places or at a later date. Under copyright law it is not necessary for them to make a drastic change to their usual *modus operandi*. They can go on negotiating a fixed fee from their 'client' but, according to the copyright method, they should now specify that this fee covers only the initial use of the translation that the client has proposed. In principle, this allows a repeat fee to be requested for any subsequent use of the translation that was not foreseen in the initial licence. It leaves the copyright in the translator's hands while providing the client with the only the specific rights he needs for his immediate purposes.

10.4.2 Benefits of TA membership

All benefits arising from membership of the Society of Authors are available to members of the TA. These include advice on negotiation, vetting of contracts and the pursuance of complaints. All advice is, naturally, both free and confidential. A model translator/ publisher contract, which is constantly under review, is also available to members free of charge. Information of general interest to all writers is supplied on a regular basis by the Society's journal, *The Author*, while the specific interests of literary translators are catered for in the TA's own publications.

Opportunities to meet and exchange views with fellow members of the profession are provided by meetings held at regular intervals throughout the year. These range from more formal talks or seminars on topics of current interest to an informal party held in the summer at the Society's premises. Meetings are frequently supported by the participation of publishers, editors, academics or members of related professions.

10.4.3 Organisation

The day-to-day management of the TA is in the hands of the TA Secretary who is a member of the TA's staff. There is also a 12-strong Executive Committee which meets approximately every three months. The Annual General Meeting takes place in the autumn and is normally followed by a talk or discussion. A principal item of business at the AGM is to elect new Executive Committee members (usually four) to replace members who, having served for a period of three years, retire by rotation.

10.4.4 Membership of the TA

Membership of the TA is by election at the discretion of the Executive Committee. The TA is a subsidiary group within the Society of Authors and no extra subscription for membership of the TA is required. There are two categories of membership which are detailed as follows.

Full TA membership

Full membership is normally restricted to translators who have had a translation of a full-length foreign work, or an equivalent amount of shorter material, published (in printed or electronic form) or performed commercially in the UK. Translators of technical work for commercial companies or public bodies may be admitted to membership if their work, though not on general sale, is published by the organisation commissioning it.

Associate TA membership

Associate membership is open to translators who have received an offer for the publication or broadcasting of a translation into English of a full-length work, or who have had occasional translations of shorter material, e.g. articles, short stories or poems, published or performed commercially. Translators who are resident in the UK and whose works have been published abroad may also be admitted to Associate membership. Associate members pay the same subscription and are entitled to the same benefits as full members.

10.4.5 Translators Association publications

The TA publishes a twice-yearly journal, *In Other Words*. It issues *Guidelines for Translators of Dramatic Works* and a *Quick Guide to Literary Translation*. The TA also maintains a database of literary translators from which it supplies details to publishers who are seeking a translator for a work that they plan to issue. A *Directory of British Literary Translators* is in preparation in conjunction with the British Centre for Literary Translation.

10.4.6 The Society of Authors and Translators Association Prizes

The Society of Authors and its Translators Association are responsible for administering certain translation prizes and awards. Entries for prizes should be submitted by the relevant publisher. The details listed for prizes were valid at the time of publication of this book (Early 2003) but the Society and TA should be contacted for current details.

10.4.6.1 Society of Author prizes

The Cholmondeley Awards for poets (£8,000 in total) were endowed by the late Dowager Marchioness of Cholmondeley in 1966. They are made on the strength of a poet's body of work and submissions are not accepted.

The Encore Award, sponsored by Miss Lucy Astor, is a prize of £10,000 for a second published novel. Closing date: 30 November. Entry by publisher.

The Eric Gregory Awards, established by the late Eric Gregory, are for the encouragement of promising poets under the age of 30 at the closing date. £24,500 is distributed on the strength of work submitted and taking into account the means of each winner. Closing date: 31 October.

The Tom-Gallon Award (£1,000) is a biennial prize for a short story. Previous closing date: 20 September 2002.

The Richard Imison Memorial Award (£1,500) is for the best dramatic work broadcast by a writer new to radio.

The McKitterick Prize (£4,000) was endowed by the late Tom McKitterick. It is given for a first novel, published or unpublished, by an author over the age of 40 at the closing date. Closing date: 20 December.

The Margaret Rhondda Award (£1,000) is a triennial award established by friends of Lady Rhondda to assist a woman journalist with a particular project. Next closing date: 20 December 2004.

The Sagittarius Prize (£2,000) is given for a published first novel by an author over the age of 60 at the closing date. Closing date: 20 December. Entry by publisher.

The Somerset Maugham Awards (£12,000 in total) were founded by the late Somerset Maugham to enable British authors under the age of 35 to enrich their writing by foreign travel. They are given on the strength of a published book. Closing date: 20 December. Entry by publisher.

The Betty Trask Prize and Awards (up to £25,000) were founded by the late Betty Trask for first novels (published or unpublished) by writers under the age of 35 at the closing date. They are for works of a romantic or traditional, but not experimental, nature. Closing date: 31 January.

The Travelling Scholarships (£6,000) are annual awards made to enable British writers to keep in touch with colleagues abroad. They are non-competitive and submissions are not accepted.

Application forms are available from the Society for each prize requiring books to be submitted. All prizes for published books are for books *first published in the UK*, and *published in 2002*.

10.4.6.2 Grants

The Authors' Foundation, with generous help from The Royal Literary Fund and Mrs Isobel Dalziel, gives grants to authors who need funding for research or to buy time (in addition to the advance) when working on a book, fiction or non-fiction, commissioned by a British publisher. Application is by letter. Closing dates: 30 April and 31 October.

The K. Blundell Trust provides grants to authors under the age of 40 to assist them with their next book. Applicants must submit a copy of their latest book and their work must 'contribute to the greater understanding of existing social and economic organisation'. Fiction is not excluded. Application is by letter. Closing dates: 30 April and 31 October.

10.4.6.3 Benevolent funds

The Authors' Contingency Fund provides grants to professional authors with short-term financial difficulties or for the financial relief of their dependants.

The Francis Head Bequest provides grants to professional authors over 35 whose main source of income is from their writing and who, through accident, illness or other causes, are temporarily unable to write.

The John Masefield Memorial Trust provides occasional grants to professional poets, or their immediate dependants, who are faced with sudden financial problems.

The benevolent funds are open only to authors for whom writing has provided a principal source of income. Application forms are available from the Society.

10.4.6.4 The Translators Association prizes

The Scott Moncrieff Prize, £1000. An annual prize for full length French works of literary merit and general interest. The original must have been published in the last 150 years. The translation must have been first published in the UK in 2002. Deadline: 20 December 2002

The Schlegel-Tieck Prize, £2,200. An annual prize for translations of full length German works of literary merit and general interest. The original must have been published in the last 100 years. The translation must have been first published in the UK in 2002. Previous deadline: 20 December 2002

The John Florio Prize, £1000. A biennial prize for full length Italian works of literary merit and general interest. The original must have been published this century. The translation must have been first published in the UK in 2002 or 2003. Previous closing date: 20 December 2003.

The Premio Valle Inclán, £1,000. An annual prize for translations of full length Spanish works of literary merit and general interest. The original must have been written in

Spanish but can be from any period and from anywhere in the world. The translation must have been first published in the UK in 2002. Previous deadline: 20 December 2002 **The Bernard Shaw Prize**, £1,000. A triennial prize for translations of full length Swedish language works of literary merit and general interest. The original can be from any period. The translation must have been first published in the UK during 2000–2002 inclusive. Previous closing date: 20 December 2002.

The **Vondel Translation Prize**, £2,000. A prize for translations into English of Dutch and Flemish works of literary merit and general interest. The translation must have been first published in the UK or the USA during the period specified (to be confirmed). Previous deadline: 20 December 2002.

The Sasakawa Prize, £2,000. A prize for translations of full length Japanese works of literary merit and general interest. The original may be from any century. The translation must have been first published in the UK in the period specified (to be confirmed). Next closing date: to be confirmed.

The **Calouste Gulbenkian Prize**, £1,000. A triennial prize for translations of works from any period by a Portugese national. Short stories and single poems are eligible. The translation must have been first published in the UK in 2002–2004 inclusive. Next closing date: 20 December 2004.

Entries for the translation prizes should be submitted by the publisher. For each entry, send three copies of the translation and three copies (which may be photocopies) of the original work to The Awards Secretary at The Society of Authors, 84 Drayton Gardens, London SW10 9SB.

Comprehensive details about the Translators Association are available from:

The Translators Association
84 Drayton Gardens
London SW10 9SB
Telephone: 020 7373 6642
www.writers.org.uk

11 Glossary of terms

'Denn eben, wo Begriffe fehlen
Da stellt ein Wort zur rechten Zeit sich ein.'
Goethe, 1749–1832

Though not exhaustive, this list explains some of the terms and abbreviations you are likely to encounter in translation and when using computers.

ambilingualism	Having an equal or complete functional competence in two languages.
ADSL	ADSL ('Asymmetric Digital Subscriber Line') is a type of DSL. It works by splitting your existing telephone line signal into two, one for voice and the other for data. ADSL technology can work at up to 8 Mbps download. The most popular services in the UK at the moment are running at speeds of 512 Kbps (approx. 9 times faster than a modem), although speeds of up to 2 Mbps can be obtained. Upload speeds are 256Kbps on all products and hence this is why it is 'asymmetric', because the download speed is different to the upload speed.
ASCII	American Standard Code for Information Interchange. This is a standard computer character set to enable data communication and achieve compatibility among different computer systems. The standard code contains 128 characters (96 of which are displayed in upper and lower case and 32 which are non-displayed control characters. The extended character set contains 254 characters which include a number of foreign language, technical and graphics characters. Both character sets are listed in the Appendix.

ASCII format	This is a very basic format for a file which does not contain enhancements that certain programs provide. Depending on how you save the file, it may contain only the characters in the basic ASCII character set. Can be useful when transferring a file from one system to another. See what facilities your word processing program offers.
backup	An additional copy of a computer file, usually on a floppy disk, as a safety measure should the original file become unusable. Most programs offer an automatic file backup option.
bilingualism	Using two languages in daily life, but not necessarily in the same context. A person can be bilingual without having a command of both languages in the same area.
BMP	A graphics format – bitmap. This is a representation of a video image. Each picture element, called a pixel, is represented by bits stored in a computer's memory.
bromide	A proprietary term used by printers for a full-size photograph of a single colour of a printed page used in the preparation of a printing plate.
bundled software	Software that is included with a hardware system at a package price.
cache memory	This is a special fast section of a computer's RAM (Random Access Memory) allocated to store the most frequently used information stored in the RAM.
CD ROM drive	Read-only optical storage technology that uses compact disks.
CD-R	Compact disk onto which information can be written and retrieved.
CD-RW	Compact disk onto which information can be written and retrieved. The information can be deleted and new information written – the disk is re-writable.
CGA	Colour Graphics Array. A bit-mapped display adapter for PCs that displays four colours simultaneously with a resolution of 200×320 pixels.
clock speed	The speed of the internal clock in a microprocessor that determines the rate at which the operations are processed within a computer's internal circuitry. The current entry level (2003) is in excess of 2 GHz.

copy	Term used to denote a quantity of text used for a specific purpose, e.g. advertising copy.
CompuServe	A proprietary Internet service provider.
dongle	A hardware device plugged into a computer that permits authorised use of a software program.
DOS	Disk Operating System. The 'ignition key' to earlier PCs.
dot matrix printer	A printer whose print head comprises a matrix of tiny pins which form a character. The greater the number of dots in the matrix, the sharper the image.
downloadable fonts	A font that needs to be transferred from the computer's hard disk to a laser printer's RAM before the font can be used.
dpi	Dots per inch. Most standard inkjet and laser printers provide a resolution of 600 dpi. The move is now towards 1200 dpi.
DRAM	Dynamic Random Access Memory (See RAM). This is a RAM chip that represents memory states using capacitors that store electrical charges.
DTP	Desk Top Publishing.
EGA	Enhanced Graphics Array. This is a colour bit-mapped graphics adapter for PCs that displays up to 16 colours simultaneously with a resolution of 640×350 pixels.
Electronic publishing	Electronic, or computerised, document production as opposed to physical document production.
EOF	An acronym for End Of File. It is useful to add this at the end of a file that is transmitted by modem as an indication that all the file has been sent.
EPS	A graphics format – encapsulated postscript
EPROM	Erasable Programmable Read Only Memory. A ROM chip that can be reprogrammed.
FDD	Floppy Disk Drive.
Field code	A predefined entry which includes data defined by the field. This may be a date insertion, the number of words in a document, or address data merged from a separate data file.
FIT	Fédération Internationale des Traducteurs.

floppy disk	A disk that can be inserted and removed from a computer. The disk on which information is stored is flexible but should still be treated with care. The capacity of a floppy disk can range from 360 KB to 1.44 MB depending on size and format.
floptical disk	A disk similar in format to a CD but which is read-writeable. The standard format has a storage capacity of 650 MB and needs a special drive on your computer. Combined CD/floptical drives are available.
footer	A repetitive text entry at the bottom of each section of a document or the entire document. Different headers can be used for the first page of a chapter and for subsequent odd and even pages.
fuzzy match	An approximate translation offered by a translation memory system. The degree of approximation is stated as a percentage. This match can be accepted and edited to produce an exact match.
galley	A strip of uncut pages provided by a printer and used for checking before making printing plates. (See bromide).
generic file	A computer file saved in a format that is readily accepted by different software.
GB (gigabyte)	The storage capacity of a device. 1 GB is equal to approximately one billion bytes (1,073,741,828 bytes) or 1000 megabytes.
grey scale	A number of shades of grey that can be recognised and reproduced within hardware or software. 256 grey shades is enough to reproduce most monographic images.
handshaking	This is a method of ensuring that one electronics device is ready to accept information from another. Used in fax machines and modems.
hard copy	A printed copy of a translation or document.
hard disk	The disk in your computer that provides bulk storage. Some hard disks are removable for security purposes.
Hayes-compatible	A term applied to modems to denote that the equipment conforms to certain commercial standards. Analogous to IBM-compatible.

Header	A repetitive text entry at the top of each section of a document or the entire document. As shown in this book, different headers can be used for the first page of a chapter and for subsequent odd and even pages.
HDD	Hard Disk Drive.
HTML	Hypertext Markup Language.
IBM-compatible	A general term applies to computers that use DOS as an operating system.
icon	A symbol used on screen to represent a computer entity or function.
ICR	Intelligent Character Recognition.
impact printer	A printer whose print head impacts against the paper that is to receive the print. Impact printers usually work in draft mode (high speed) where the level of resolution is sufficient for draft work and in quality mode (slower speed) for higher-resolution output. (See dot matrix printer and NLQ).
	The use of impact printers is used primarily when printing on continuous stationery in applications such as invoice or statement printing.
inkjet printer	A printer that emits a jet of ink in matrix form to produce the required character on a sheet of paper.
IoL	Institute of Linguists.
ISDN	Integrated Services Digital Network.
ITI	Institute of Translation and Interpreting.
justification	The manner in which multiple lines of text are arranged in relation to a margin. Text can be left, centre, right or full justified. This chapter of the book is printed left justified to avoid the wider gaps that can occur between words in narrow columns if the text is full justified. The rest of the book is full justified.
KB (kilobyte)	The storage capacity of a device. 1 KB is equal to approximately one thousand bytes (1024 bytes).
LAN	Local Area Network. Computers linked within a limited area by high performance cables to enable information interchange, shared hardware resources and which use a powerful secondary storage unit called a file server.

language of habitual use	A language that is used habitually. This may not be your mother tongue.
laser printer	A high-resolution printer that uses electrostatic reproduction technology to form the required characters. (See postscript printer).
LCD	Liquid Crystal Display. A device that uses crystal molecules that change their orientation when a current flows through them.
LED	Light Emitting Diode. This is an electronic component that gives off light when a current flows through it.
localisation	Modification and presentation of a text in a form that suits the local market or user.
Macintosh	A type of computer that has its own operating system but which is not directly compatible with IBM-compatible computers.
masthead	This is the section of a newsletter or magazine that gives details about staff, ownership, advertising, subscription etc.
MB (megabyte)	The storage capacity of a device. 1 MB is equal to approximately one million bytes (1,048,576 bytes). 1 MB is 1000 kilobytes.
Microsoft Windows	A windowing environment and user interface used to operate PCs in a similar manner to Macintosh.
MIPS	A unit used for measuring the rate at which a computer executes instructions. 1 MIP = 1 Million Instructions Per Second.
modem	MOdulator/DEModulator. A piece of equipment that converts computer file information to a form that can be readily transmitted via a telephone line and received and demodulated by compatible equipment.
monitor	That part of your computer that displays the information with which you are working. Also called the screen.
mouse	A piece of equipment that attaches to your computer and allows you to move a pointer around the screen and perform file processing activities. (Plural: mice, generic term: rodents).
natural language	This is a term used to differentiate a naturally-occurring language (such as English, French or German) from a computer programming language.

NLQ	Near Letter Quality. A level of quality achieved by impact printers.
OCR	Optical Character Recognition. This is a technique for recognising printed text using computer software. The graphic shapes of characters are matched up to internal tables and the corresponding ASCII text is derived from them.
ODA	Office Document Architecture.
OEM	Original Equipment Manufacturer.
on-line	A program or device that is connected directly to a computer and which is available while using a program application.
parallel port	A port that enables synchronous, high-speed flow of information along parallel lines to peripheral devices such as printers.
pixel	Picture element.
postscript printer	A laser printer that provides a range of fonts in different sizes. The camera-ready copy for this book was printed using a Hewlett Packard 2000C inkjet printer with a resolution of 600 dpi.
PROM	Programmable Read Only Memory. As the name implies, this is a read-only memory chip.
proof	A final copy of a text or document submitted for approval.
RAM	Random Access Memory. In simple terms, this denotes the operating capacity of your computer.
resolution	The minimum size of dot that can be produced by a scanner or printer. The higher the resolution, the sharper the image will appear. Resolution is usually expressed in dots per inch (dpi). The majority of current laser printers provide a resolution of 600 dpi.
RIP	Raster image processor.
ROM	Read Only Memory. Part of a computer's primary storage that is not volatile.
RSI	Repetitive Strain Injury. An injury that develops after continuously repeating the same physical action, e.g. keyboarding.

scan checking	A level of checking whereby the checker ensures that all the required text has been translated and makes spot checks to ascertain quality.
scanner	A device that scans and digitises an image (graphics or text) so that it can be merged with a word processing or DTP package.
screen saver	This is a utility that blanks off your computer screen when not in use in order to save energy and prolong the life of your monitor.
serial port	A port that synchronises and enables synchronous communication between a computer and peripherals such as serial printers and modems.
SGML	Standard Generalised Markup Language
SIMM	Single Inline Memory Module.
soft copy	A document provided on a computer disk. (See hard copy).
software piracy	The unauthorised copying and use of copyrighted software.
source language	The language from which you translate.
spell checker	A module within most standard word processing packages to check the spelling of words or detection of unrecognised groups of characters. This is not a substitute for proof checking.
Style sheet	A set of formatting instructions that can be applied while word processing to ensure consistency of layout. Headings to which styles have been applied can be used to generate a list of contents at the beginning of a document automatically.
SVGA	Super Variable Graphics Array.
TA	The Translators Association of the Society of Authors.
T switch	A switch that is used to direct two or more sources (e.g. computers) to a single output (e.g. printer).
target language	The language into which you translate.
tagged files	Files which are marked or 'tagged' for formatting in a specific software program.
Toolbar	A set of icons displayed in the upper section of your computer screen and which can be used to invoke specific functions defined by the program in use at the time.

translation memory	An integral part of computer-aided translation systems. It is the information stored in the translation memory that is retrieved, and edited where appropriate, and inserted in a new translation.
turbo	An option provided on some computers to enhance processing speed.
virus	An undesirable set of computer instructions that can corrupt information on your computer. The results can be devastating.
VDU	Visual Display Unit. Another term applied to a computer screen or monitor.
VGA	Video Graphics Array.
volatile data	Data that is no longer stored if you leave a software program or switch off your computer.
WYSIWYG	What You See Is What You Get. A screen display that approximates to what will be printed on paper. Earlier software that did not display directly in WYSIWYG usually had a page view facility that offers the same display.

12 Appendix

12.1 Translation organisations in the United Kingdom

The Institute of Linguists
Saxon House
48 Southwark Street
London
SE1 1UN

Tel: 020 7940 3100

The Institute of Translation and Interpreting
Fortuna House
South Fifth Street
Milton Keynes
MK9 2EU

Tel: 01908 325250

The Translators Association of the Society of Authors
84 Drayton Gardens
London
SW10 9SB

Tel: 020 7373 6642

Association of Translation Companies
Alexandra House
Alexandra Terrace
Guildford

Surrey
GU1 3DA

Tel: 01483 456486
www.atc.org

A comprehensive directory of translator organisations, addresses and descriptions are given in:
 Edwards J.A., and Kingscott A.G., (1997) *Language Industries Atlas 2nd Edition*, IOS Press Amsterdam.

12.2   Recruitment competitions

Where to write for information on translation recruitment competitions:

The European Community
INFO-RECRUITMENT
Recruitment Unit
Commission of the European Communities
rue de la Loi 200
B–1049 Brussels

The United Nations

(Candidates living in Europe)
Secretariat Recruitment Section
(Competitive Examination for English Translators/Précis-writers)
Room 266
United Nations Office at Geneva
CH–1211 Geneva 10
Switzerland

(Candidates living outside Europe)
Recruitment and Placement Division
(Competitive Examination for English Translators/Précis-writers)
Office of Human Resources Management
Room S-2535E
United Nations Secretariat
New York, N.Y. 10017
United States

12.3 Suggested further reading

I have not referenced these books in the accepted manner since the reader will probably be interested in what a book is about rather than a specific author.

Business and marketing

Lloyds Bank Small Business Guide, 1999 Edition, Sara Williams, Penguin Books, 426 pp, ISBN 0–14–0127721-B.

Nick Robinson's Marketing Toolkit, Nick Robinson, 1991, Mercury Books, 202 pp, ISBN 1–85252–038–8.

Everything you need to know about marketing, Patrick Forsyth, 1990, Kogan Page Ltd, 126 pp, ISBN 1–85091–945–3.

Perspectives on electronic publishing, Sandy Ressler, 1993, PTR Prentice-Hall, 343 pp, ISBN 0–13–287491–1.

Mind your manners. Managing Business Cultures in Europe, New Edition, John Mole, 1998, Nicholas Brealey Publishing, 236 pp, ISBN 1 85788 085–4.

Language, translation and interpreting

Careers using languages, Edda Ostarhild. Ninth edition. Kogan Page. 2002. ISBN 0749437316 .

12.4 References

1. Landers C.E., (2001) *Literary Translation – A Practical Guide*, Multilingual Matters Ltd.
2. Phelan M., (2001) *The Interpreter's Resource*, Multilingual Matters Ltd.
3. Dalby, D., (1997) *The Linguist*, Vol 36, No 5, p.142
4. Smith, M., (1998) *The Financial Times*, January 3/4, p.1
5. Paraswaman, A. *et al.,* (1985) A conceptual model of service quality and its implications for further research. *Journal of Marketing.*
6. Ansoff, H. I., (1968) *Corporate Strategy*, Penguin. Harmondsworth
7. Samuelsson-Brown G. F., (1996) *Working Procedures, Quality and Quality Assurance* in Owens R. A. Ed. *The Translators Handbook*, ASLIB. p.110
8. BS 4755: 1971. 'Specification for the presentation of translations'
9. BS 5261: Part 2: 1976. 'Copy preparation and proof correction'
10. ISO 2384–1977 (E). 'Documentation – Presentation of translations'

12.4.1 ASCII Standard Character Set

The appropriate characters can be obtained by pressing the Alt key and the relevant code numbers (on the numeric keypad) at the same time.

ASCII number	Character	ASCII number	Character	ASCII number	Character
033	!	065	A	097	a
034	"	066	B	098	b
035	#	067	C	099	c
036	$	068	D	100	d
037	%	069	E	101	e
038	&	070	F	102	f
039	'	071	G	103	g
040	(	072	H	104	h
041	)	073	I	105	i
042	*	074	J	106	j
043	+	075	K	107	k
044	,	076	L	108	l
045	-	077	M	109	m
046	.	078	N	110	n
047	/	079	O	111	o
048	0	080	P	112	p
049	1	081	Q	113	q
050	2	082	R	114	r
051	3	083	S	115	s
052	4	084	T	116	t
053	5	085	U	117	u
054	6	086	V	118	v
055	7	087	W	119	w
056	8	088	X	120	x
057	9	089	Y	121	y
058	:	090	Z	122	z
059	;	091	[	123	{
060	<	092	\	124		
061	=	093	]	125	}
062	>	094	^	126	~
063	?	095	_		
064	@	096	`		

ASCII number	Character	ASCII number	Character	ASCII number	Character
129	ü	171	½	213	Õ
130	é	172	¼	214	Ö
131	â	173	¡	215	×
132	ä	174	«	216	Ø
133	à	175	»	217	Ù
134	å	176	°	218	Ú
135	ç	177	±	219	Û
136	ê	178	²	220	Ü
137	ë	179	³	221	Ý
138	è	180	´	222	Þ
139	ï	181	µ	223	ß
140	î	182	¶	224	a
141	ì	183	·	225	ß
142	Ä	184	¸	226	G
143	Å	184	¹	227	p
144	É	186	º	228	S
145	æ	187	»	229	s
146	Æ	188	¼	230	m
147	ô	189	½	231	t
148	ö	190	¾	232	F
149	ò	191	¿	233	Q
150	û	192	À	234	W
151	ù	193	Á	235	d
152		194	Â	236	¥
153	Ö	195	Ã	237	f
154	Ü	196	Ä	238	e
155	¢	197	Å	239	Ç
156	£	198	Æ	240	º
157	¥	199	Ç	241	±
158	_	200	È	242	³
159	ƒ	201	É	243	£
160	á	202	Ê	244	ó
161	í	203	Ë	245	õ
162	ó	204	Ì	246	‚
163	ú	205	Í	247	»
164	ñ	206	Î	248	°
165	Ñ	207	Ï	249	×
166	ª	208	Ð	250	×
167	º	209	Ñ	251	Ö
168	¿	210	Ò	252	_
169	_	211	Ó	253	2
170	Ø	212	Ô	254	n

12.5 Marking up texts when proof-reading or editing

There is a British Standard which illustrates all the standard proof marks used. This is 'Copy preparation and proof correction', BS 5261: Part 2: 1976. Extracts from this standard are reproduced with the kind permission of BSI. Complete copies of the standard can be obtained from:

Address: 389 Chiswick High Road, London, W4 4AL, United Kingdom
Telephone: +44 (0)20 8996 9000 www.bsi-global.com

General

Instruction	Mark in text	Mark in margin	Notes
End of correction	None	/	To be made after each correction
Leave unchanged	_ _ _ _ _ _ under characters to remain unchanged	✓	
Refer to translator if anything is of doubtful accuracy	Encircle word(s) affected	?	It is also possible to mark 'OK?' in margin instead of the mark specified

Deletion, insertion, substitution

Instruction	Mark in text	Mark in margin	Notes
Insert at the mark in text the matter indicated in the margin	ʌ	New matter followed by ʌ	
Insert additional matter identified by a letter in a diamond	ʌ	ʌ followed by, for example, ⟨A⟩	This is to be used if the matter to be added cannot comfortably be written in the margin and requires additional space ⟨A⟩

Deletion, insertion, substitution (continued)

Instruction	Mark in text	Mark in margin	Notes
Delete	/ through individual character(s) or ⊢————⊣ through words or parts of words to be deleted	ℐ	
Delete and close up	ℐ through individual character(s) or ⊨====⊨ through words or parts of words to be deleted	ℐ	
Substitute character or substitute part of one or more words	/ through individual character(s) or ⊢————⊣ through words or parts of words to be deleted	New character or word(s)	
Change to capital letters	≡≡≡≡ under character(s) to be changed	≡	If space does not permit, encircle the character(s) to be changed instead
Change to bold type	∼∼∼∼ under character(s) to be changed	∼∼	
Change capital letters to lower case letters	Encircle character(s) to be changed	≢	

Deletion, insertion, substitution (continued)

Instruction	Mark in text	Mark in margin	Notes
Substitute or insert superscript character	/ through character or ⋀ where required	⋎ under character e.g. ²⋎	
Substitute or insert subscript character	/ through character or ⋀ where required	⋀ over character e.g. ⋀₂	
Substitute or insert full-stop or decimal point	/ through character or ⋀ where required	⊙	

Note that the above instruction can be applied to the substitution or deletion of other punctuation characters.

Positioning and spacing

Instruction	Mark in text	Mark in margin	Notes
Start new paragraph	⌐⌐	⌐⌐	
Run on (no new paragraph)	⌒	⌒	
Transpose characters or words	⎿⎤ between characters or words, numbered where necessary	⎿⎤	

177

Positioning and spacing (continued)

Instruction	Mark in text	Mark in margin	Notes
Centre	⌈ enclosing matter ⌉ to be centred	[ ]	
Indent			Indicate the amount of indent in the margin
Cancel indent			
Move matter a specified distance to the right	enclosing matter to be moved to the right →		Indicate the exact dimensions if necessary
Move matter a specified distance to the left	← enclosing matter to be moved to the left		Indicate the exact dimensions if necessary
Take character(s), word(s) or line over to next line, column or page			The mark in the text surrounds the matter to be taken over and extends into the margin
Take character(s), word(s) or line back to previous line, column or page			The mark in the text surrounds the matter to be taken over and extends into the margin
Move matter to position indicated	Encircle matter to be moved and indicate new position		Show exactly where the matter is to be moved to
Correct vertical alignment	‖	‖	

Positioning and spacing (continued)

Instruction	Mark in text	Mark in margin	Notes
Correct horizontal alignment	Single line above and below misaligned letter(s)	═══	The mark in the margin is placed level with the top and bottom of the relevant line
Close up/delete space between characters or words	link͡ing	⌒	
Insert space between characters	| between characters affected	Y	Indicate the size of the space to be inserted if necessary
Insert space between words	Y between words affected	Y	Indicate the size of the space to be inserted if necessary
Reduce space between characters	| between characters affected	T	Indicate the amount by how much the space is to be reduced if necessary
Reduce space between words	between T words affected	T	Indicate the amount by how much the space is to be reduced if necessary
Make space appear equal between characters or words	| between characters or words affected	Ⴢ	
Close up to normal interline spacing	(each side of column linking lines)		The marks in the text extend into the margin

Positioning and spacing (continued)

Instruction	Mark in text	Mark in margin	Notes
Insert space between lines/paragraphs	or		Indicate size of space to be inserted where necessary
Reduce space between lines or paragraphs	or		Indicate the amount of the reduction if necessary

Below is an example of a text containing common errors and the relevant proof marks, and the corrected text.

The text is a photocopy taken directly from a brochure where the translation into English was made by a person who did not have English as his language of habitual use.

[ ] OUR ~~DELIVERY PROGRAM~~ *RANGE OF SERVICES/*

∧ U/

INJECTION MOLDING TOOLS All ~~kinds for thermo and duroplastic~~. *⊢ types of thermoplastics and thermosetting resins/*

FORGING TOOLS All ~~kinds~~ forging die. *⊢ types of/*

PUNCHING TOOLS All ~~kinds~~ cutting, punching, *⊢ types of/* bending, forming and stamping tools.

EXTRU~~DING~~ TOOLS Nozzles for tubes and foil. *⊢ SION/*

AUXI~~U~~ARY TOOLS Jigs and fixtures. */ L I/*

PRESSING AND CASTING TOOLS For rubber, polyurethan~~ ~~ *∧e/* structure foam, and ligt alloys. */ a I/ ∧h/*

SPECIAL MACHINES According to customer's specifications.

PROTO~~/~~PRODUCTION Prototypes for ~~mechanical~~ *∧ TYPE/ /d'/* industry as well as plastic and wooden patterns. *⊢ the engineering/*

SUB~~/~~CONTRACTING Small and medium batches based upon ~~universal mechanical production~~. *∧-/* *⊢ a broad range of production equipment./*

OUR RANGE OF SERVICES

INJECTION MOULDING TOOLS	For all types of thermoplastics and thermosetting resins.
FORGING TOOLS	All types of forging die.
PUNCHING TOOLS	Cutting, punching, bending, shaping and stamping tools.
EXTRUSION TOOLS	Dies for tubes and foil.
AUXILIARY TOOLS	Jigs and fixtures.
PRESS AND CASTING TOOLS	Tools for rubber, polyurethane, structural foam and light alloys.
SPECIAL MACHINES	According to customer specifications.
PROTOTYPE PRODUCTION	Prototypes for the engineering industry, as well as plastic and wooden patterns.
SUB-CONTRACTING	Small and medium-sized batches based on a broad range of production equipment.

This is a good example of the difficulties that confront the translator when faced with text laundering. The original Norwegian language original was fortunately available otherwise it would have been difficult to try to interpret what the writer had intended. Even so, it would have been useful to speak to the author to hear what he had intended.

13 Index